# SEVEN SONGS
# OF CREATION

# SEVEN SONGS OF CREATION

## LITURGIES FOR CELEBRATING AND HEALING EARTH

An *Earth Bible* Resource

## NORMAN C. HABEL

THE
PILGRIM
PRESS
Cleveland

The Pilgrim Press
700 Prospect Avenue
Cleveland, Ohio 44115-1100
pilgrimpress.com

© 2004 by Norman C. Habel

All rights reserved. Published 2004

Printed in the United States of America on acid-free paper

08   07   06   05   04          5   4   3   2   1

**Library of Congress Cataloging-in-Publication Data**

Seven songs of creation : liturgies for celebrating and healing earth : an Earth Bible resource / Norman C. Habel, [editor].
     p.  cm.
   Includes bibliographical references.
   ISBN 0-8298-1593-7 (pbk.)
   1. Worship programs.  2. Season of Creation – Prayer-books and devotions – English.  3. Creation – Prayer-books and devotions – English.
4. Earth – Prayer-books and devotions – English.   I. Habel, Norman C.
BV135.S43S48 2004
265'.9 – dc22
                                                    2004044601

# CONTENTS

**Part Two**
**EARTH SONGS**

## Part Three
## ADDITIONAL RESOURCES

# PREFACE

This collection, an *Earth Bible* resource, contains seven liturgies for celebration and healing. It has been a privilege during the past few years to work with numerous creative people in preparing this volume. The Spirit has been stirring us to develop new forms of worship that connect us with Earth and all our kin in Earth community. Earth has been a living presence among us, stimulating us to listen, to empathize, to sing, and to heal.

I hope these seven liturgies will provide the impetus for us all to revere, honor, love, and serve Earth in a fresh and dynamic way. Whether used in a liturgical Season of Creation or periodically — as times and circumstances dictate — these liturgies are creating a new way to understand the way we worship God. The liturgies are not concerned with making Earth the theme of worship. Rather, they attempt to create a way of worshiping with Earth and joining with water, with forests, with all living creatures, to worship and celebrate our God, who in Jesus Christ became a piece of Earth for us and with us.

So my gratitude is extended not only to many friends from differing denominations who contributed to the total collection of materials, but also, and especially, to Earth and all the images, presences, powers, and songs of Earth that impinged upon our consciousnesses to create these worship materials.

Individuals and groups who contributed to the liturgical resources are acknowledged at the end of each liturgy; the groups participating in this project include the Sophia Community, the Creation Theology Group, the South Australian Council of Churches, the Ecotheology e-mail group, and the Oshkosh Worship Group. Numerous individuals also made valuable contributions to the form and content of these materials.

My special thanks to Doug Petherick, who drafted the music into its appropriate format, and to Joh Wurst, who functioned as a critical editor familiar with healing rites.

Finally, this project owes a special debt of gratitude to the Charles Strong Trust, the Adelaide College of Divinity, and Flinders University.

The Trust continues to fund this project as a direct offshoot of the Earth Bible Project; without the support and financial assistance from the Trust, neither project would have been more than a fond dream, a cherished wish in the hearts of the creative minds participating in the projects, and an unfulfilled vision of a new possibility for being an Earth community in relationship with each other and with God and a worshiping community that spans the universe.

While many of these worship materials were developed in Australia, the great majority reflect a worship context far beyond our southern shores "on the bottom of the world." From my location "down under," however, let me extend a favorite local blessing:

> May the Spirit
> surprise you
> like a dove
> from above,
> or a swallow
> from below,
> but now and then
> as a blue wren.

# INTRODUCTION

## RESPONSIBLE RELATIONSHIPS

Earth is facing an environmental crisis. This crisis threatens the very life of the planet. The atmosphere we breathe is being polluted. The forests that generate the oxygen we need to survive are being depleted at a rapid rate. The fertile soils we need to provide food are being poisoned by salinity and pesticides. The waters that house organisms essential to the cycle of life are being polluted by chemicals and waste. Global warming has become a frightening threat. The list goes on.

The crisis facing Earth is more than an environmental issue. It is about more than scientific understandings and biological interdependencies and symbiotic connections, more than facts and figures about sustainable levels of pollution and tolerable levels of toxicity. Essentially, this crisis is about responsible relationships. Human communities that are intended to live in harmony with creation are exploiting Earth and destroying other species in Earth community. Human communities that are intended to be agents who care for creation are greedy and arrogant, ruled by economic rationalist thinking and "acceptable levels" of abuse. Global economics continue to subject Earth to destructive strategies euphemistically called "development." According to Jürgen Moltmann, this crisis is "the beginning of a life and death struggle for life on this Earth."[1]

This environmental and economic crisis is no longer one that Christians can ignore as irrelevant to our mission as church, as body of Christ, as children of God, and as a priesthood of believers. The mission of the Christian church has traditionally been understood as tending the spiritual welfare of human beings. In popular terms that mission involved "saving souls." For some Christians, more recently, the mission of the church is being understood differently. This new understanding of mission is focused on making human lives whole and liberating oppressed communities from the forces of death and destruction.

---

1. Jürgen Moltmann, *God in Creation: An Ecological Doctrine of Creation* (London: SCM, 1985), xi.

11

Now Christians face a third mission: healing Earth. Christians are now called to be agents of healing and hope for Earth. Christians have a responsibility to care for Earth rather than view it as a piece of disposable matter ready for the wastebasket of eternity. Earth is not just another planet. Earth is a sacred site in the cosmos, a planet chosen by God as the locus of life in all its majesty and mystery. Even more significant, perhaps, is that God has chosen to fill this planet with God's presence and glory. Earth is a sanctuary and we, as Christians, are summoned to revere the Earth and to work with Christ to restore its full fruitfulness and flourishing.

## CREATION LITURGIES

Where and how do we begin this mission? Worship is one vital starting point! Through worship we have an opportunity to create a deeper consciousness of the crucial task before us. Our mission is spiritual and relational, not just environmental and political. This mission of healing Earth involves deep transformations in thinking, doing, and ways of being; it is not about "being seen to be doing the right things." To heal Earth we need to connect again with God at work creating our planet, Christ at work reconciling all things in creation, and the Spirit at work renewing Earth.

We also need to connect with Earth as sanctuary, as spiritual home, as sacred garden of God, as place where God chooses to become one with us through incarnation and sacrament. We need to listen to the voices of creation in our worship: voices of lament and praise, voices of solidarity and resistance. We need to expand our expression of worship to include celebrating with Earth, with Earth community and with all creation. We need to expand our worship to include listening to God's voice speaking to us through God's word — words of affirmation and caution — and through the voices of those who are being oppressed and abused, who cry out against what human beings do to each other and to other members of Earth community we share. The liturgies in this collection are intended to help us open our minds to, and link our spirits with, the wider worshiping community of creation.

Many traditional Christian liturgies have a few lines that include this wider worshiping community, but most Christian worship takes place inside buildings with walls and windows that are not see-through, that serve to exclude God's creation, that focus our eyes of faith away from Earth community. A few flowers on the altar barely evoke a sense of presence of forests where the community of all creation is praising their creator. The eyes of worshipers are generally directed heavenward. Many hymns have a focus on heaven. For example, "Guide me, O thou great Jehovah, pilgrim through this barren land," tends to devalue Earth as a "barren land." Many of us have sung these words in the context of worship without thinking about their implicit and explicit messages to us and their effect on our relationships with Earth community.

All the contributors to this text — as writers and composers, as readers and responders to written words and ideas, as catalysts for insights and understandings — believe that through these "Seven Songs of Creation," human worshipers value rather than devalue Earth and revere rather than exploit creation. We also believe that these liturgical resources can help us each to discern what celebrating our creator God together with other members of our Earth worshiping community means for how we think, what we believe, and how we act. These liturgies are designed to help us worship with creation and, in so doing, celebrate the presence of God in creation. The liturgies are designed to help us become agents of Christ in the mission of healing creation and collaborators with the Spirit in renewing creation.

## INTRODUCING A SEASON OF CREATION

If we are to be serious about our commitment to this task of healing the Earth, we need to do more than participate in a creation liturgy on Earth Day or join with our children in blessing animals, birds, fish, gardens, and fields. We need to introduce a new season into our church worshiping program. We need a Season of Creation: a sustained sequence of worship that enables us to focus on a particular aspect of our understanding of God's participation in our lives on Earth. We need a Season of Creation to experience worship with the wider Earth community, to appreciate the sacredness of Earth, and to grasp the tragic consequences of what humans have done to God's sanctuary: God's garden of delights and re-creation.

In recent times, some people have suggested weeks of the church year that could be allocated to a Season of Creation. One suggestion we find most appealing is the period of five weeks that culminates in the festival of St. Francis of Assisi in early October. Using five liturgies from this volume, we recommend the following sequence for a Season of Creation, building to the *Song of Healing* on the Festival of St. Francis.

**A Season of Creation:**

Week one: ***Song of Sanctuary***

Readings: Isaiah 6:1–3
Psalm 97
John 1:1–16

Week two: ***Song of Earth***

Readings: Genesis 1:1–25
Matthew 27:50–54; 28:1–6
Romans 8:18–25

Week three: ***Song of Sky***

Readings: Psalm 19
Isaiah 54:6–11
John 3:1–8

Week four: ***Song of Waters***

Readings: Psalm 104:24–34
Romans 6:1–4
John 9:1–11

Week five: ***Song of Healing***

Readings: Job 38:1–11; 39:5–12
Genesis 1:26–28; 2:4b–10, 15
Mark 10:41–45
Revelation 22:1–4

Two additional liturgies, *Song of Sophia* and *Song of Life*, are included for use on special occasions. The first is a feminist liturgy that celebrates the vibrant presence of Sophia (Wisdom) in creation. The second celebrates the life of Earth using the Song of Songs in a creative and sensitive way. In particular communities these liturgies could replace weeks three or four in the suggested Season of Creation.

During this Season of Creation, some groups may wish to gather for worship in natural settings outside buildings — in forests or hills, beside lakes or on the seashore, in the bush or a garden. Alternatively, the worship space inside the church building could be transformed imaginatively to suggest a garden, a rain forest, a stream, or a mountaintop. The key is to use symbols to evoke a particular domain of creation as part of the worshiping experience.

## THE *EARTH BIBLE* CONNECTION

Behind these liturgies is the research and approach connected with the *Earth Bible*.[2] The five volumes of the *Earth Bible* series seek to develop strategies for reading Scriptures afresh, from the perspective of Earth.

A few years ago, some of us who consider the Bible an important source of wisdom in society as well as church life decided to reread the Bible in the light of the ecological crisis. We also decided to be honest with the entire text and not to indulge in "cherry picking" — that is, selecting only those texts that are obviously Earth friendly.

How were we to reread the text — any text anywhere in the Bible — in the face of the current ecological crisis? Our first step was to engage in serious dialogue with ecologists to gain a deeper understanding of the issues. What were the governing principles of ecology that might guide our investigation? And what kind of approach would we follow if we took these principles into account? The following six ecojustice principles were formulated to guide a reader reading from the perspective of Earth.

- **The principle of intrinsic worth:** the universe, Earth, and all its components have intrinsic worth/value.

- **The principle of interconnectedness:** Earth is a community of inter-connected living things that are mutually dependent on each other for life and survival.

- **The principle of voice:** Earth is a subject capable of raising its voice in celebration and against injustice.

- **The principle of purpose:** the universe, Earth, and all its components are part of a dynamic cosmic design within which each piece has a place in the overall goal of that design.

- **The principle of mutual custodianship:** Earth is a balanced and di-verse domain where responsible custodians can function as partners

---

2. I have chosen to italicize *Earth Bible* because it is a shortened form of the "Earth Bible Project," and "The Earth Bible" five-volume series edited by Norman C. Habel and published by Sheffield Academic Press and The Pilgrim Press.

with, rather than rulers over, Earth to sustain its balance and a diverse Earth community.

- **The principle of resistance:** Earth and its components not only suffer from human injustices but actively resist them in the struggle for justice.

Reentering a text from a new direction[3] and with new eyes was not easy. We had all been reading with old habits, old ways of finding the meaning in the text. We had been seeing things from the perspective of our respective human cultures. Could we change our lenses and begin to read from the perspective of Earth? Could we read as members of an Earth community rather than simply as members of a human community?

With the above principles in mind and identifying with Earth and the wider Earth community, we asked these key questions as we read the scripture texts from the perspective of Earth:

- Is Earth valued for itself or only as a resource for humans?

- What role does Earth play as a character in the story?

- Is the voice of Earth heard or suppressed in the story?

- Does Earth suffer unjustly at the hands of God or humans?

Even though the Bible is a text inspired by God, we were ready to face the possibility that many texts in the Bible, written as they are by humans, are likely to be human-centered and relegate Earth to the margin. We were aware that in the history of interpreting the text, we have often been so concerned about getting to heaven that we have considered Earth unimportant, disposable, and even a barren "vale of tears." We were also ready, however, to discover texts where the value, mystery, sacredness, and wonder of Earth and Earth community is explicit or implicit, but has been ignored or hidden precisely because human-centered questions have dominated our approach to reading the text.

The *Earth Bible* Project resulted in the publication of five volumes of readings, written by biblical scholars and Bible readers from diverse cultural and linguistic backgrounds and regions and scattered across six

---

3. The concept is Adrienne Rich's. See Rich, *On Lies, Secrets and Silence* (London: Virago, 1979), 35.

continents of our planet. The first volume, *Readings from the Perspective of Earth*, provides context for the project and sample readings reflecting a range of strategies. The other volumes in the series focus on sections within the Bible and include: *The Earth Story in Genesis*, *The Earth Story in Wisdom Traditions*, *The Earth Story in Psalms and Prophets*, and *The Earth Story in the New Testament*.

Throughout this book we have capitalized "Earth." This is to emphasize that we are focusing on Earth as a living subject, a planet whom God has chosen to make a sanctuary.

## ORIGINS

The liturgies in this collection emerged over a period of three years. Quite independently, several writers who were included in the *Earth Bible* series discerned the need to express their spiritual insights and new Earth-consciousness in their worship practices. The specific context that inspired a liturgy is noted in the "Setting" section of each liturgy.

While the *Earth Bible* Project was located in Australia, the writers involved — and the worshiping communities for which the liturgy was written — are scattered across the globe. In the final selection of seven liturgies, we sought to be broadly representative of the denominational, cultural and linguistic diversity and religious heritage reflected in the five volumes of the *Earth Bible* series. These are the origins of each of the liturgies:

**Song of Sanctuary:** rural — Uniting Church in Australia

**Song of Earth:** ecumenical — Council of Churches, South Australia

**Song of Sky:** ecumenical — Native American links

**Song of Waters:** ecumenical — ecotheology enthusiasts, Australia

**Song of Sophia:** ecofeminist — Sophia Community, Adelaide, South Australia

**Song of Life:** ecofeminist — Creation Spirituality, United States of America

**Song of Healing:** international — Lutheran World Federation

# FORMAT

Each of the seven liturgies in Part One of this volume is presented in the same format. An introductory section, "Setting," describes the focus, setting, and the context that led to the development of each liturgy. The symbols and imagery associated with the motif (governing theme and subject) of the liturgy are also introduced in this section.

An extended section called "Text and Reflection" follows. This section serves two purposes: to provide the biblical basis for the particular form and focus of the liturgy, and to take into account some of the findings of our *Earth Bible* research. This section also provides textual material for the preacher or celebrant who wishes to explore the relevance of the theme for the life of the worshipers. The translations are the original work of writers and biblical scholars who have participated in developing the liturgy.

The section titled "Liturgy" contains the worship order for each liturgy. Each liturgy included in this volume focuses on at least one major domain or dimension of creation. These liturgies are designed to facilitate a worship experience that not only creates a fresh awareness of the presence of God in and with creation, but also stimulates a consciousness that Earth and the wider Earth community are members of the worshiping community praising and serving God the creator.

One of the ways to recognize that human beings are part of a wider worshiping Earth community is to allow domains and beings of creation to be heard in worship. If we follow the lead of the psalmists (e.g., in Psalm 148), all members of Earth community have voices. They may not have human voices, but they cry out to God in pain or praise. The voices of Earth, mountains, forests, and other domains of creation can be heard in praise, lament, or dialogue with humans in these seven liturgies. In our view, it is vital for human beings to listen to the voices of Earth community. In this respect, we can learn from Indigenous peoples around the world who, unlike most Western Christians, are still sensitive to the voices of creation.

Part Two, *Earth Songs*, contains a selection of new songs and hymns. Some of these have been written to reflect readings included in the *Earth Bible* series or the insights of ecology and other creation-focused sciences, and the spiritual and faith-life understandings of a growing Earth consciousness among contemporary Christians. Seven of the songs are theme songs, each focusing on the theme and motifs of a particular liturgy. Some lyrics have been written to be used with well-known melodies, resulting in a creative tension evocative of our current explorations in ecotheology: the tune evokes a previous consciousness, while we sing aloud words reflecting our new understandings of our place in Earth community. Musicians are welcome to compose alternative melodies for these songs.

Additional worship resources relating to the themes and emphases of these liturgies are provided in Part Three of this volume. These worship resources include alternative prayers, litanies, blessings, confessions, reflections, and related materials developing themes and motifs of particular liturgies.

Several of the liturgies do not include a Eucharist. Worshiping communities are invited to integrate a Eucharist into every liturgy. A special text for "A Healing Eucharist" is provided on p. 197.

## HEALING EARTH

In the course of preparing and testing these liturgies, we became aware of the need to focus on how participants can move from the worship setting into their every day roles as members of Earth community. A number of the liturgies include rituals of commitment where worshipers promise to counter the crimes against creation and prevent them in the future. A practical way to undergird this act of commitment in a given community is to refer to appropriate local issues in the liturgy and encourage participants to be actively involved in local, regional, and global programs that support environmental justice and restoration.

We also became aware that if we think about and relate to Earth and Earth community as fellow worshipers — as suffering and celebrating with us on this planet — we need to include them as participants in need of healing. Practices and rites of healing differ in Christian communities. In traditional liturgies, healing is an integral and implicit part of the Eucharist: worshipers understand and have faith in the healing power of Christ's body and blood. In some worshiping communities, the laying on of hands is part of the Eucharist: a human action to focus the recipient's faith on this healing power.

In developing healing rites for Earth and Earth community, we had few precedents to guide us. We can, of course, pray that the healing power of the Eucharist be mediated through human worshipers to every domain of Earth. This is premised on the understanding of humans as priests for all creation, mediating God's healing to all. *Earth Bible* readings remind us that Christ has come to redeem humanity and to restore all creation (Ephesians 1:9–10; Colossians 1:15–20).

We pray for the healing of Earth at various points in each of the seven liturgies. In the *Song of Healing,* the final liturgy, however, we incorporate a rite of healing for Earth. In this ritual activity, worshipers become the healing hands of Christ in the world. It is our hope that this rite will provide a precedent for other rituals that focus on healing the wounds of Earth and all members of Earth community, as well as the hurts of humans.

## THE EARTH CHARTER

One of the signs of an emerging Earth consciousness in the world is the Earth Charter. While this document is not explicitly religious, it embraces a broad spirituality that has enabled people from diverse faiths and traditions across the globe to be part of its preparation for submission to the United Nations. Its very first principle is to "respect Earth and life in all its diversity." For details about the Earth Charter visit www.earthcharter.org.

Included in this volume is a song entitled "One Earth" (p. 182), which was launched and sung as part of the 2001 Asia Pacific Earth Charter Conference. This song reflects the values and hopes for Earth reflected in the Earth Charter.

A commitment to Earth written by Anjali Habel-Orrell in collaboration with other young people in 2000 is included below and reflects the vision of the Earth Charter. This commitment could be included in each of the liturgies as a promise not only to Earth but also to our God and creator who is the source of all life, and to Christ the redeemer of all life, and to the Spirit who works to renew all creation.

## We Promise Earth: A Commitment to Earth

We, the youth of the world
recognize that we have exploited Earth.
But from now on

**we promise Earth**
that we will respect all life-forms,
and celebrate them
as valued members of Earth community.

**We promise Earth**
that we will care for Earth
as Earth cares for us;
that we will protect Earth community from harm,
and preserve its resources so that future generations
will have the healthy food, air, water, and soil they need
to live full lives.

**We promise Earth**
that we will struggle to overcome those forces
that keep members of Earth community
poor, oppressed and excluded.

**We promise Earth**
that we will support ways of improving life
and ensuring a better future for all
by using all Earth community resources to sustain life,
rather than exploit it.
**Yes, we promise the Earth.**

We hope that these liturgies, songs, and resources will inspire you not only
to praise your Creator but to join in worship with Earth and all creation.

# Part One

# LITURGIES

# ONE

# SONG OF SANCTUARY

## Earth says:
## "I am the chosen sacred site
## in your corner of the cosmos."

### SETTING

*Song of Sanctuary* highlights the biblical revelation that Earth is a sacred place, a planet filled with God's presence, a special sanctuary in God's cosmos. The Word that emphasizes this revelation is taken from Isaiah 6:1–3 and linked with John 1:14. In the rites of this song of creation we are invited to make connection not only with God as Creator, but also with Earth as that place where God chooses to dwell and with human flesh as that being God became in Jesus Christ.

The liturgy is designed to raise our consciousness of Earth as sacred home of God and human beings, to celebrate God's presence among us in Earth, to confess how we have desecrated this sanctuary, and to find ways of reconnecting with, and healing, Earth. It is especially through the healing power of Jesus, the Wisdom and healer of creation, that we are united again with Earth as our sacred source of daily life. Earth is more than just a stopping place en route to heaven or a limitless landscape of resources to be exploited and consumed as disposable goods. Earth is a sanctuary to be revered as our human home and God's abode. Being alive involves being interconnected with Earth, the substance from which we were created, according to Genesis 2. As a tangible reminder of this connection, when our bodies die, the water and other substances that comprise our physical being are returned to Earth: our bodies are totally biodegradable, and our reintegration into Earth is seamless.

The focal symbol for worship in this liturgy, as in most of the other liturgies in this collection, is an Earth bowl, the symbol of Earth and its bounty. The Earth bowl is a large round clay bowl filled with soil, placed on a pedestal. In *Song of Sanctuary*, this bowl may be surrounded by trees and other live plants. Plants and trees in pots may also be placed throughout the worship space as appropriate. At the center of the bowl is a candle or red glowing light representing the glory of God that fills Earth. A special rite for reconnecting with Earth is also included to assist worshipers to relate again to Earth as a sacred and living place, a place to be revered and respected for its own sake.

This liturgy was originally developed for a community of rural worshipers who wished to experience the presence of God and the sacredness of Earth in their part of the Australian countryside.

As a direct outcome of this worship experience, the group plans to replace at least the front of their place of worship with a wall of glass so that God's presence in creation can be experienced visually during their worship.

## TEXT AND REFLECTION

### Texts

The reflection that follows sets the scene for celebrating *Song of Sanctuary*. This study explores the biblical background and environmental context of this liturgy, especially Isaiah 6:1–3. This reflection aims to help human worshipers sing "Song of Sanctuary" with a fresh awareness of God's awesome presence in Earth and of Earth as a sacred planet.

The reading from the Gospel of John is closely connected to the revelation of Isaiah 6 that Earth is filled with God's glory. In John's Gospel prologue, the writer announces that when the Word becomes flesh we behold God's glory. The glory of God that can be seen in Earth is, according to the writer of John's Gospel, focused in one piece of Earth: the flesh called Jesus Christ.

Norman Habel translated the texts from the Bible included in this liturgy.

### Isaiah 6:1–3

*In the year that King Uzziah died, I saw YHWH God sitting on a throne, high and lofty, and the hem of God's robe filled the temple. Seraphs were in attendance above; each had six wings: with two they covered their faces, with two they covered their feet, and with two they flew. And one called to another and said:*

> "Holy, holy, holy is YHWH God of hosts,
> All of Earth is full of God's glory."[1]

## Reflection, by Norman Habel

### Past Readings

The story of Isaiah's call in Isaiah 6 has often been used to motivate Christians to pursue mission work. Christians are summoned to reply with Isaiah: "Here am I, send me!" The text has been understood to mean that Christians should go into distant lands to preach God's Word. These readers did not seem to pause and ask what the bold announcement of God's amazing messengers that "Earth is full of God's glory" might mean. They were concerned about saving souls for heaven, not about the implications of the song of God's glory filling Earth for all life to experience.

Time and again many of us have sung a version of this song from Isaiah as the Sanctus in worship. The version many of us remember reads:

> Holy! Holy! Holy, Lord God of hosts!
> Heaven and Earth are full of your glory.

You will notice that in this version "heaven" has been added to the text of Isaiah. The result is that many of us do not appreciate the full force of the original text. In Isaiah 6, it is not heaven but Earth that is full of God's glory. In fact, it is the heavenly beings, the seraphim, who are singing antiphonally that all of Earth is full of God's glory. And that is the message of the text that we want to explore in this liturgy.

What does it mean for Earth to be full of God's glory?

### Reading the Text Again

To appreciate the significance of this text we first need to recall the story of God's glory in the history of God's people, Israel. In Exodus 16, the people of God who escaped from Egypt complained that they faced starvation in the wilderness. God promised them manna from heaven but also appeared as a dazzling cloud filled with fire. That fire cloud was God's glory, a visible expression of God's presence with them on their journey.

God's glory was visible again on top of Mount Sinai as a great cloud filled with a fierce fire (Exodus 24:17).

---

1. On the use of "YHWH" see "The Text" on p. 59.

God's glory appeared again when the tabernacle had been completed and, as the text reports, God's glory filled the tabernacle (Exodus 40:34–38). God's glory was the visible presence of God filling the tabernacle. In the same way, the visible glory of God filled the holy of holies in the temple that Solomon built in Jerusalem (1 Kings 8:1–11).

When we read the text of Isaiah 6:3 closely what do we discover? The YHWH God of the heavenly hosts may be holy, but where is the visible presence of God to be seen? Throughout Earth! Earth is filled with God's glory like the tabernacle and the temple at Jerusalem! That is what Isaiah hears the seraphim cry out. In the past, God's glory may have been seen only in certain sacred places on Earth, such as in the tabernacle, in a fire cloud, on Mt. Sinai, or in the holy of holies of the temple in Jerusalem. Isaiah, however, makes it clear that God's glory may be seen throughout Earth. Earth is filled with the glory of God!

## Earth as God's Sanctuary

What then is the significance of this revelation? First of all it means that just as the tabernacle and the temple were sanctuaries of God's glory, signifying God's presence, Earth is also a sanctuary of God's glory, God's visible presence. God, it seems, has chosen Earth as that planet in the whole cosmos to fill with a sacred pulsating presence: God's glory. Earth is much more than a ball of water, dirt, and air spinning through space. Earth is God's sanctuary; Earth is a sacred site in the cosmos; Earth is filled with God's presence.

If Earth is indeed God's sanctuary, filled with the presence of God, then we have opportunities to see God's presence all around us. We are living in God's chosen planet and are surrounded by God's presence. If we open our eyes of faith to behold the clouds, forests, and rocks anew, we will see God's visible presence in Earth. We will see God's glory in Earth — it is the soil as well as the sunset, the fronds of a fern as well as the eyes of a lion, the whale song and the gnat's buzz.

If Earth is indeed God's sanctuary, then we also have the responsibility to keep it sacred and prevent it from being desecrated. Human beings should be priests rather than polluters of God's sanctuary, Earth.

By looking honestly at what humans have done throughout Earth, we can see the reality of human desecration.

## Sacred Lands Desecrated

We have polluted God's sanctuary in many ways — with toxins, blood-shed, waste. One of the worst ways we have desecrated God's sanctuary is through our experiments with nuclear energy and its by-products: waste, explosions, and pollution through accidental leaks. Nuclear materials have half-lives longer than many generations of human beings; nuclear waste, in human terms, lasts forever. The genetic damage of the Hiroshima-Nagasaki "experiment" will have consequences for more than ten generations!

Let us consider one local example of our irresponsible fascination with nuclear energy.[2]

In Australia there is one place where, I am ashamed to say, we desecrated vast tracts of land, land that belonged to Indigenous Australians. This land was their homeland, and it was filled with their sacred places.

After the Second World War, the local Australian government wanted to please their British "mates" and allies, and help, as it said, "to keep the free world free." So the government agreed that the then so-called "mother country" could test atomic bombs at a place in the center of Australia called Maralinga. They said it was okay because the land was "empty" except for a few Indigenous people. And they could easily be moved somewhere else, as they had done nothing to "improve" these tracts of land, and to the white officials one piece of barren land was the same as any other to these "uncivilized" peoples.

Although the government officials tried to evacuate all the Indigenous Australians living there before they exploded the bombs, they did not find them all. And all life-forms and land-forms in these areas were contaminated. Aboriginal Australians both inside and outside the prohibited zone were exposed to radioactive contamination and fallout. Some recall a "black radioactive cloud" that brought sickness and death. The "red sands," of which the Indigenous Australians were proud and with which they had a spiritual bond, became "poisoned" and gray. Their animal and plant kin were contaminated. Their sacred sites — rocks, landforms, water holes — were contaminated. These sacred lands at the center of Australia were contaminated, and God's sanctuary — God's Earth — was desecrated. And Earth still cries out in pain. Even after more than fifty

_____
2. In other contexts, local examples may be more appropriate.

years, and attempts at decontamination, the land is irretrievably polluted, and the genetic contamination will continue for generations.

There are similar stories about how Earth and members of Earth community have been desecrated in other parts of the globe. In the twenty-first century, with global access to information, they are only too familiar sources of pain and shame for many of us.

### The Masks of God

A feature of this liturgy is a reflection on the masks of God. The expression "masks of God" (*larvae dei*), is derived from sixteenth-century German theologian Martin Luther. Luther was a highly educated Catholic monk, whose ninety-five theses, outlining practices within the existing Christian church tradition that Luther perceived needed to be reviewed in the light of the Christian Gospel, are credited with beginning the Protestant breakaway from the then dominant Western Christian tradition, Catholicism.

According to Luther, the face or presence of God is in all creation—but it is hidden, masked from human eyes. In Luther's understanding of the Isaianic revelation that Earth is filled with God's presence as God's glory, nature both masks and reveals God's presence in creation. For those who can see—through the eyes of faith—the presence of God, indeed, God's face, can be seen in, with, and under all creation, including the bread and wine of the Eucharist. For those who do not have faith, creation masks God's face; Earth is just a piece of dirt, water, and rock floating in space; creation is expendable and can be abused and discarded; the bread and wine of the Eucharist are just bread and wine.

# LITURGY: SONG OF SANCTUARY

**Song:** "Song of Sky" (p. 150)

### Invitation to Worship

*The invitation to worship should be called, sung or shouted from a distant point, whether a hill, a treetop, or the open door of a church before anyone enters the worship place. Worshipers may then enter holding bright flowers or branches to celebrate the beauty of our living Earth.*

Leader          Come, enter the sanctuary of God,
                     the sanctuary called Earth.

| All | We will enter the sanctuary of God,<br>and celebrate with creatures of Earth,<br>with wombats and wolves and crocodiles,<br>with parrots, green tree frogs, volcanoes,<br>and white waterfalls. |
|---|---|
| Leader | Come, enter the sanctuary called planet Earth,<br>filled with the glory of God. |
| All | We enter. We wonder!<br>We enter and see all the mysteries of Earth:<br>molecules, whales, and orchids,<br>fossils, earthworms,<br>and delicate wild sea horses. |
| Leader | Come, enter the sanctuary called Earth,<br>and behold the glory of God. |
| All | We enter, we watch —<br>and behold God's glory throughout Earth:<br>on the rain forest floor,<br>in the red desert flower,<br>in the green sea coral,<br>in gleaming beach sands. |
| Leader | Come, revere the glory of God<br>in the delicate web called creation. |
| All | We come and revere.<br>We stand still in awe<br>at the intricate Earth that we share:<br>the snowflakes that link us with clouds;<br>the soil that links us with trees and plants;<br>the elements that link us with lava;<br>and the atoms that link us with ants. |
| Leader | Come, celebrate in the sanctuary of God,<br>in this sacred site of God's cosmos. |
| All | Earth is full of the glory of God.<br>We live in the presence of God. Amen. |
| Refrain | Holy! Holy! Holy, YHWH God of space.<br>Planet Earth is full of your glory! |

## Readings

**Reading 1**     Isaiah 6:1–3

**Reading 2**     Psalm 97

**Reading 3**     John 1:1–14

### *Response to the Readings*

*This response may be whispered by several readers — with pauses between paragraphs — and should be accompanied by appropriate background music or Earth sounds.*

Voice 1     Perhaps we dare not view the face of God unfiltered,
            the glaring intensity of life itself.
            So across planet Earth God leaves
            a million masks...
            veils shielding the glory
            to protect those with eyes to see.

Voice 2     For masks may reveal —
            as well as conceal —
            the pulsating presence of the Spirit creating,
            of Wisdom at play...

Voice 3     When we see God in Jesus Christ —
            God robed in human dust —
            our eyes are opened to see God
            wherever there is dust and soil: the good stuff of creation.

Voice 4     In the flesh of that mortal,
            we see God's glory — in the flesh:
            not in the fantastic, but in the clay;
            not in the celestial, but in the forest;
            not in the cathedral, but in a tiny seed.

Voice 5     Now we can see God's glory
            incarnate everywhere
            in the sanctuary of God
            called planet Earth.

All         *Jesus Christ, help us to see*
            *the glory of God in you,*

wearing the flesh and blood and clay
we wear every day.
Help us to see the glory, the face of God
around us in all creation. Amen.

**Song:** "Hear This Earth Mourning" (p. 178)

## Confession: Two Clouds

*The leader should pause after each statement from the group to allow time to reflect on the implications of our desecrating God's sanctuary, Earth.*

| | |
|---|---|
| Leader | Deep in the desert<br>the fire cloud emerged —<br>and the glory of God was visible<br>to the people of Israel: men, women, and children. |
| *All* | *Deep in the desert*<br>*we drilled for oil —*<br>*and clouds made of fumes*<br>*can be seen above our cities,*<br>*polluting the air.* |
| Leader | High on the mountain<br>the fire-cloud settled and shone,<br>and Moses entered the fire<br>to meet God face to face. |
| *All* | *High over mountains*<br>*clouds of smoke from forest fires rise,*<br>*as millions of acres are burned*<br>*in the Amazon and Indonesia.* |
| Leader | In the midst of the temple<br>the fire-cloud filled the holy of holies —<br>a sign of God's presence. |
| *All* | *In the midst of the daylight*<br>*clouds of polluting toxins*<br>*have filled the atmosphere*<br>*of God's sanctuary*<br>*and obscured God's presence.* |

| Leader | Once God's people beheld God's glory |
|---|---|
| | and were amazed. |
| | They entered God's sanctuary |
| | and knew God was there. |

| All | *Now we, God's people, have hidden God's glory.* |
|---|---|
| | *We have desecrated God's sanctuary;* |
| | *and we are ashamed.* |

*Additional acts of desecration may be confessed by concerned worshipers. After each confession the people respond with the words below.*

| All | *Forgive us and help us, Creator God.* |
|---|---|

**Song:** "Song of Sanctuary" (p. 146)

**Reflection**

*The reflection included in the previous section may be used, or an alternative reflection, written for the local context, may be used as a sermon or in the form of drama. Discussion may also be used here.*

## Rite for Reconnecting with Earth

*At the center of the worship space is an Earth bowl — a large round low earthen or clay bowl placed on a pedestal, containing loose soil, representing Earth. At the center of the bowl is a candle or glowing red light representing the presence/glory of God in Earth. In addition, trees and plants may be placed around the Earth bowl, and scattered throughout the worship space.*

### The Blessing

| Leader | Before us is the Earth bowl, |
|---|---|
| | filled with soil from our place on this planet, |
| | soil that is the very stuff of life, |
| | the clay of our creation. |

| All | *As we bless this soil today,* |
|---|---|
| | *we bless Earth and honor planet Earth as sacred.* |

| Leader | We bless this soil |
|---|---|
| | in the name of the Creator who |
| | brought Earth forth from the deep; |

in the name of Jesus Christ who became clay —
one with Earth and one with us;
and in the name of the Spirit
who breathes new life to Earth each dawn.

All        *Amen.*
*May Earth always be a sacred place for us.*

## The Sharing

*The leader moves to stand before the Earth bowl and invites worshipers to come forward in groups to connect again with Earth by placing their hands together in the Earth bowl and symbolically sharing their connection with the soil that unites all creation.*

Leader      I invite you now to come forward in groups
to the center of this sacred space.
I invite you to come to the soil at our center
and connect once again with Earth.
Earth invites you to come back home
and connect with your origins as Earth matter.

All        *Creator God, bring us home,*
*and help us recognize we are one with Earth.*

*As groups come forward, music may be played and songs sung. The following invitations and responses are made to each group at the bowl.*

Leader      I invite you to sense the presence of Earth,
and the presence of God filling Earth.
I invite you each to affirm that you are one with Earth.

All        *Creator God, bring us home,*
*and help us recognize we are one with Earth.*

Leader      I invite each of you now
to take a handful of soil and share it
by pouring it into the hands of those near you
while saying:
One with Christ,
One with Earth.

*Worshipers come forward and form a circle. The leader takes a handful of soil, hands it to one person who in turn hands it to the next person in the circle saying: "One with Christ, One with Earth." The final person returns the soil to the Earth Bowl. The ritual sharing of the soil of Earth is like sharing the peace of Christ. After all in the group have shared their connection with Earth, the leader dismisses the group with the following words, and the group responds before leaving the bowl to return to their places.*

Leader      May our sharing of Earth help us express
our deep bond with Earth
and share Earth's goodness with all in need:
people, animals, birds, plants, insects — all creation.

All      *Thank you, Creator God, for reconnecting us with Earth.*

**Song:** "God's Sacred Secret Garden" (p. 174)

## Eucharist

*A loaf of freshly baked bread placed in a bowl or basket and a recently opened bottle of wine are carried in during the song and placed on the soil in the Earth bowl.*

Leader      God the Creator be with you.

All      *And also with you.*

Leader      Open your eyes and see God's glory around us.

All      *We see that God's glory fills Earth.*

Leader      Let us celebrate in God's sanctuary, Earth.

All      *We celebrate our Creator God with all creation.*

Leader      It is indeed right that we should celebrate your sanctuary,
YHWH God, our Creator,
For you chose this planet to be your sanctuary —
a sacred space in the cosmos
where you are present in a special way.
Your glory fills Earth with fire,
fills grain with goodness,
and fills grapes with blessing

|  |  |
|---|---|
|  | for us to celebrate |
|  | as we sing the song of your sanctuary: |
| Refrain | Sanctus (p. 165) |
| All | *Holy, holy, holy, YHWH God of space.* |
|  | *Planet Earth is full of your glory!* |
| Leader | We acknowledge your presence, YHWH God, in Earth: |
|  | in the colors of the landscape — |
|  | the crimson of the flower, |
|  | the red of the clay, |
|  | the glowing flames of a bushfire, |
|  | and the golden glow of the falling star. |
| All | *We remember your fire in the burning bush,* |
|  | *your glowing thundering glory on Sinai,* |
|  | *your glory cloud in the temple,* |
|  | *and the fire-cloud with your people in the wilderness.* |
| Leader | But especially we acclaim your glory |
|  | in Jesus Christ our wise healer — |
|  | God in the flesh, |
|  | exposing your glory in human form, |
|  | in flesh, bone, and blood. |

*The leader blesses the elements in the manner appropriate to the tradition of the worshipers, while breaking the bread and pouring the wine into the cup and saying the words of institution.*

|  |  |
|---|---|
| Leader | We remember the night when you were betrayed, |
|  | You took bread, broke it, and said, |
|  | "This is my body, which is given for you." |
|  | After supper you took the cup, gave thanks, and said, |
|  | "This is the blood of the new covenant, |
|  | which is shed for you for the forgiveness of sins. |
|  | Do this as often as you drink it, in remembrance of me." |
| All | *Open our eyes to see your glory,* |
|  | *open our hearts to know your love,* |
|  | *open our souls to sing the Song of Sanctuary* |
|  | *with Earth and all creatures of Earth —* |
|  | *a song to celebrate your presence in this place,* |

*and in every place on our planet,*
*here and now, today. Amen.*

*The leader and assistants distribute the bread and wine while saying, "The body of Jesus Christ, given for you," and "The blood of Jesus Christ, shed for you." After the distribution, the leader says the following words to the group.*

| | |
|---|---|
| Leader | May the body and blood of our Lord<br>strengthen your faith in Jesus Christ,<br>and strengthen your bonds with Earth,<br>the source of your own body and blood. |
| All | *Amen.*<br>*We are one in Jesus Christ;*<br>*We are one with Earth.* |

**Song:** "Song of Healing" (p. 166)

**Commitment**

*Special prayers for the day, Earth and the crises of Earth, may be said. The prayers should be followed by the rite of commitment.*

| | |
|---|---|
| Leader | Let us commit our lives to our Creator God<br>in the service of Earth. |
| All | *YHWH God, we choose this day*<br>*to walk on Earth as holy ground,*<br>*your sanctuary in the cosmos.*<br>*We pledge not to desecrate Earth,*<br>*but to revere, respect, and love Earth*<br>*as a fertile and fragile home,*<br>*your sanctuary, filled with your presence.*<br>*We promise to serve Earth,*<br>*tilling, tending, and touching its soil*<br>*as we would those we love and respect. Amen.* |
| Leader | As a tangible sign of your commitment, you are invited to take consecrated soil from the Earth bowl, and join it with soil in a place that is special, that is sacred for you — in your garden, in the bush, or some other place that you choose. Although the whole of Earth is God's |

sacred place, set this place apart to remind you, every day, that Earth is God's sanctuary.

## Closing Blessing

Leader      As you leave this place,
May your feet fall softly
on the holy ground
of Earth, God's planet sanctuary,
shared with us as a home.
May your eyes discern
God's face in the soil of your garden
and in the new leaves of a tree.
May you catch now and then
the dance of the Spirit
in the bouncing play of a puppy
and the lilting song of a gentle blue wren.

All      *We will walk and watch and wonder.*

Leader      May Earth, filled with God's glory
be holy for you every day.

All      *And also for you.*

Leader      Go in peace and serve Earth in celebration!

All      *Amen.*

*As worshipers leave, they walk past the Earth bowl. They take an envelope from a basket placed nearby and place in it some sacred soil from the Earth bowl. They take it away with them and add it to the soil in a place that becomes especially sacred and reminds them that Earth is God's sanctuary.*

# T W O

# SONG OF EARTH

### Earth says:
### "I wasn't created; I was revealed."

## SETTING

This liturgy focuses on Earth as a unique revelation. Earth is more than another created object: Earth "appears" from beneath the waters in Genesis 1; Earth is revealed when God speaks. Earth is at the center of the creation story in Genesis 1. And when this Earth story is complete God cries, "Very good!" — or, even better, "Wonder-full!" And Earth is alive: in response to God's word all kinds of fauna and flora appear and flourish.

The wonder of this story is expressed visually by using seven stations of creation. At the center of the worship space is a large bowl filled with soil. This "Earth bowl" is the focal point: it is the symbol of Earth revealed, Earth polluted, and Earth restored. Each of the other seven stations, whether located at the front of the worship space or at points around that space, is marked by a lighted candle and a symbol of one of the seven days of creation. The following are suggested symbols for the seven stations:

Station 1:   a large crystal or similar object that reflects light

Station 2:   feathers from flying birds

Station 3:   seeds and soil of Earth

Station 4:   sunflowers

Station 5:   large sea shells and sand

Station 6:   animal figurines, preferably made from clay

Station 7:   musical instruments and a book.

40

The symbols listed are only suggestions. Any symbols representing the specific days of creation that are meaningful to a particular worshiping community may also be used. However, as day six focuses on the life that emerges from Earth rather than on humans (who some believe were created to "rule" Earth), the symbol chosen should not represent human beings.

Corresponding to the seven days of creation are seven days of destruction. As each human act of destruction is confessed, the candle from the appropriate station is placed in the Earth bowl and extinguished. At the end of service, the worshipers remember the day of resurrection and make seven promises to work with Earth to restore the planet. With each promise, a candle is lit and replaced at the appropriate station of creation.

## TEXTS AND REFLECTION

### Texts

This translation of Genesis 1 was developed by Dr. Norman Habel while working with the Rainbow Spirit Elders, Indigenous Australians who have a close kinship with Earth and land.[1]

Suggested additional biblical readings are Matthew 27:50–54, 28:1–6; and Romans 8:18–25. These readings are located at appropriate points in the liturgy. The first reading emphasizes that Earth is a sympathetic participant in the death of Christ, the second that Earth suffers and groans in anticipation of rebirth, and the third that Earth is involved in celebrating the resurrection of Christ.

### Genesis 1

*In the beginning*

> *In the beginning,*
> *when God created sky and Earth,*
> *Earth was unformed and empty;*
> *darkness was upon the face of the deep,*
> *and the spirit of God glided over the face of the waters.*

---

1. Another version of this translation appears in a work entitled *The Rainbow Spirit in Creation: A Reading of Genesis 1* (Collegeville, Minn.: Liturgical Press, 2000). In this text, the various sections of the reading correspond to a set of ten paintings that portray the events of creation through Indigenous symbols and art work.

Light

> And God said, "Let there be light!"
> And there was light.
> God saw the light was good.
> And God split the darkness with the light.
> God called the light Day
> and the darkness Night.
> It was evening and morning.
> DAY ONE.

Sky

> And God said let there be a canopy
> in the midst of the waters,
> and let it split the waters.
> So God made the canopy
> and split the waters that were under the canopy
> from the waters that were above the canopy.
> And it was so.
> God called the canopy sky. It was evening and morning.
> DAY TWO.

Earth

> And God said, "Let the waters under sky
> be gathered together in one place,
> and let the ground be revealed."
> And it was so.
> God called the ground Earth
> And the waters that were gathered together
> God called sea.
> And God saw it was good.

Vegetation

> Then God said, "Let Earth bring forth vegetation:
> plants that produce seeds,
> every species of fruit tree that bears fruit with a seed in it on Earth."

And it was so.
Earth brought forth vegetation:
every kind of plant that produces seeds,
and every species of tree that produces fruit with a seed in it.
God saw that it was good.
It was morning and evening.
DAY THREE.

Sun and Moon

And God said, "Let there be lights in the canopy of sky
to split day and night.
And let them be for signs and seasons, days and years.
And let there be lights in the canopy of sky
to provide light on Earth."
And it was so.
God made the two great lights,
the greater light to rule the day,
the lesser light to rule the night, and the stars.
And God saw that it was good.
It was morning and evening.
DAY FOUR.

Birds and Sea Life

And God said, "Let the waters bring forth swarms of living things,
and let birds fly over Earth across the canopy of sky."
God also created great sea monsters
and every species of living thing that swarms in the waters
and every species of winged bird.
And God saw that it was good.
God sang them and said,
"Be fruitful and multiply and fill the waters in sea,
and let the birds multiply on Earth."
It was evening and morning.
DAY FIVE.

*Animals*

> And God said, "Let Earth bring forth every species of living creature:
> cattle and creeping things and wild life on Earth."
> And it was so.
> God made every species of wild life on Earth,
> and every species of cattle,
> and every creeping thing on the ground.
> And God saw that it was good.
> DAY SIX.

*Rest*

> So sky, Earth, and their company were completed.
> On the seventh day God completed the work to be done,
> and rested on the seventh day from the work that was done.
> God sang the seventh day and made it sacred,
> because on it God rested from all the work of creation to be done.
> This is the family story about when sky and Earth were created.

## Reflection, by Norman Habel

### Preamble

This reflection sets the scene for the liturgy entitled *Song of Earth* (pp. 48, 152). It explores briefly the biblical background and environmental context of the song. This reflection aims to help us sing "Song of Earth" with a fresh awareness of Earth's wonder and mystery, to develop a readiness to revere this wondrous place called Earth, and to desire to work with Earth to restore pristine beauty.

### The Text: Genesis 1:1–2, 9–13, 24–25

> In the beginning, when God created sky and Earth,
> Earth was unformed and empty;
> darkness was upon the face of the deep,
> and the Spirit of God glided over the face of the waters.
> And God said, "Let the waters under sky be gathered in one place
> and let the ground appear." And it was so . . .
> And God called the ground Earth.
> And the waters that were gathered together God called sea.

*And God saw it was good...*
*Then God said, "Let Earth bring forth vegetation:*
*plants that produce seeds, every species of fruit tree*
*that bears fruit with a seed in it on Earth"...*
*And God said, "Let Earth bring forth every species of living creature,*
*cattle and creeping things and wild life on Earth."*
*And it was so... and God saw that it was good.*

## Past Readings

The story of Genesis 1 has been told over and over again. It has been read as the basic text for the church's teaching on creation. It has been interpreted by some scholars seeking to disprove evolution. Still others have viewed the text as poetry or myth, a sacred story about the origins of the universe. But few have recognized that central to the text is the story of Earth's origin and fertility.

For many of us the story of creation that we learned in church is an account of how an all-powerful creator, existing alone by "himself," chose to create the cosmos out of nothing. Nothing existed. Over six days God said "Let there be" several times and with each announcement something new came into being. God was like a cosmic boss giving orders. God spoke and things came into being: light, sky, Earth, vegetation, sun, living creatures, and humans.

If, however, we read the text more closely and focus on Earth as a central character in the story we discover new things. What we want to explore in this study is the question: "Who is Earth in the Genesis 1 story of creation?"

## Reading the Text Again

As you begin to read Genesis 1, try to identify with Earth as a main character in the story. Where is Earth at the beginning? How is Earth described? Notice that Genesis 1:2 begins by telling us the condition of "the ground" whom later God calls "Earth." The key character in the story, apart from God, is Earth.

So, who is Earth?

We can say at least three things about Earth at the beginning. First, Earth was "unformed and empty." The text does not say Earth did not exist, but that Earth was empty. Second, Earth was in darkness, unseen and hidden. Third, Earth was lying beneath deep waters that needed to be removed for Earth to be seen. Who is Earth? A mysterious, hidden, unformed presence waiting to be revealed.

So what was necessary for Earth to be uncovered, seen and filled? First of all light! Without light Earth could not be seen when it appeared. Second, the waters hiding Earth had to be removed. This removal of the deeps happens in two stages: first, a canopy, called sky, is constructed to hold back one body of waters. The waters in sky are there to provide rain and sustenance for Earth when it appears.

In the second stage, God summons the rest of the waters to separate so that Earth may appear. At this dramatic moment Earth is revealed. This is the first climax in the story. God says, "Let the ground appear." The text does not say, "Let there *be* ground," or "Let there *be* Earth." Why? Because the ground that God names Earth has been a presence below the waters waiting to appear. The full force of this dramatic appearance of Earth becomes clear when we realize that the Hebrew word for "appear" is the very same word used when God or an angel appears. If we call an appearance of God a "theophany," we might call this appearance of Earth a "geophany." Like God, Earth is revealed. Who is Earth? A revealed presence.

The story continues when God addresses Earth and calls on Earth to bring forth life-forms from deep within. First Earth brings forth all kinds of vegetation, all species of tree and plant. Later the waters of Earth bring forth swarms of sea creatures (Genesis 1:20). And finally (Genesis 1:24–25), Earth brings forth every species of living creature, from crawling insects to wild beasts of the rain forests. Once again, God does not simply say, "Let there be cows and other creatures"; God calls to Earth to bring them forth from itself. Who is Earth? Earth is the source of all living beings, the source whom God summons to bring forth life.

### Earth as Mother

One of the remarkable aspects of this story is that Earth is a partner in the creation story. Earth is a mother: Earth brings forth all forms of life. God honors Earth by calling on Earth to become the mother of all life, to bring forth all biotic forms of life from within, from the womb. If God so honors Earth, surely we should do the same.

God does more than honor Earth in this way. God also responds to Earth when Earth is revealed. God looks at Earth, and all other creatures, and God discovers that they are "good." God does not make them good but discovers that they are good. In other words, God looks at Earth and is delighted, amazed. When God sees Mother Earth — and all the life that emerges from Mother Earth — God rejoices (Psalm 104:31). Who is Earth? Earth is God's partner in the creation process whom God honors and celebrates.

## Raping Mother Earth

We have all become aware that many parts of Earth have been exploited, polluted, desecrated, and devastated by human lust and folly. One of the last frontiers on Earth is Siberia, a vast domain where we might expect to find landscapes and species free from the ravages of human greed. In September 1995, the cover of *Time Australia* magazine pronounced, "The Rape of Siberia." The lead article quotes Alexei Yabloko, a leading Russian ecologist, as saying:

> Let's say you decide to get away from it all in Siberia. You travel up the Yenisey River toward the Arctic. You look across the empty tundra and think you are alone in nature, miles upon miles from the nearest person, and you decide to stretch out on the riverbank. Unfortunately, you are lying on sands contaminated by plutonium from three upstream nuclear reactors whose radioactive wastes have been dumped for over 40 years.

The rape of much of Siberia includes not only nuclear waste, but also air pollution with numerous poisons, devastation of vast forests, and elimination of rare species. Some of the remaining peoples, like the Udege, turn to tiger poaching to survive. The story of Siberia, sad to say, is repeated many times over in many parts of Earth.

## Preparing for Worship

As we prepare for worship, we are invited to honor Earth as God did. We are invited to rejoice in Earth and the fertility of Earth. We are invited to celebrate Earth as our Mother and our future. We are invited to look at Earth, as God did, to discover, be amazed, and wonder at all the mysteries that link us together as part of the ecosystem called Earth. Before beginning the liturgy, select one or more people to be the Earth chorus. The songs they will sing are found in Part Two, "Earth Songs."

# LITURGY: SONG OF EARTH

## Invocation

Leader  God, our Creator,
who rolled back the waters of chaos
to reveal God's Earth,

     Jesus Christ,
who became earthy human flesh
to reveal God's love on Earth,

     Holy Spirit,
who opens our eyes to creation
to reveal God's presence on Earth,

All    *Open our eyes and our hearts*
*to discover the wonders of Earth,*
*the mysteries of creation,*
*and your presence deep within.*
*Amen!*

## Reflection

*The focus of this liturgy is on the story of Earth in Genesis 1 and the response of Earth at the resurrection. Central to the creation theme in this liturgy is the celebration of "Earth revealed" as depicted in Genesis 1:9–10. The text of the Reflection given above (p. 44) may be shared here or used as a bulletin insert. You may want to write your own reflection on Earth revealed.*

**Song:** "Morning Has Broken" (Traditional; can be found in most hymnals)

**Invitation to Praise** (A Version of Psalm 148)

Leader  Mother Earth, who once rose —
a majestic glistening orb,
from the dark primal waters,

All    *Celebrate your birth with us!*

Leader  Molten rocks rising from the ocean floor
and breaking through the swelling waves,

               colliding continental plates thrusting upward
               to form great mountain chains across the land,

**All**           *Celebrate your breakthrough with us!*

**Leader**     Flooding rains and swirling winds,
               gentle breezes and trickling streams,
               weathered peaks and alluvial plains,
               alive with the creating spirit of Earth,

**All**           *Celebrate your spirit with us!*

**Leader**     The green of spring and the gold of autumn,
               the cool rain forest and the warm atmosphere,
               the soil that sustains and the water that revives,
               and the blessing of Earth that is life itself,

**All**           *Celebrate your life with us!*

**Leader**     Fragile Earth, delicate web,
               intricate world, wild and wonderful,
               resisting the forces of destruction,
               and rising new each dawn from the deep,

**All**           *Celebrate with us!*
               *Rise again with us!*
               *Rejoice with us!*

## Reading

**Reading 1**     Genesis 1:1–25

## Litany

A Gloria Sung with God: And God saw all that God had made and God said, "Wonderful!"

**Leader**     When light breaks soft across the dawn,
               When light splits clouds and thunder cracks,
               When light unveils its colors in a bow,

**All**           *Show yourself to us, good Earth,*
               *as once you did long ago,*
               *when God first saw you and said, "Wonderful!"*

| | |
|---|---|
| Leader | As sky envelops us with blue, <br> As the storm clouds explode around us, <br> As fresh air invades our bodies, |
| All | *Show yourself to us, good Earth!* |
| Leader | Like the first island emerging green, <br> Like the first shoots breaking the surface, <br> Like the first life-form evolving free, |
| All | *Show yourself to us, good Earth!* |
| Leader | Where the waves break on silver shores, <br> Where the edge of land touches sea, <br> Where the sand sings with the surf, |
| All | *Show yourself to us, good Earth!* |
| Leader | In deserts where eagles soar, <br> In the bush where wallabies hide, <br> In the rivers where trout surprise, |
| All | *Show yourself to us new again, good Earth,* <br> *as you did once long ago* <br> *and we will sing with God:* |
| Earth chorus | Song: "Wonderful" (p. 187) |

WONDERFUL!
This Earth is wonder-full!
God's chosen place!
A soul in space!
Alive! Alive! Alive!
And wonder-full!
WONDERFUL!

**Song:** "Song of Earth" (p. 152)

**Readings**

**Reading 2**    Matthew 27:50–54

**Reading 3**    Romans 8:18–25

## Confession

*A candle and a symbol representing one of the days of creation is located at each of the seven stations around the church as described in the Setting section of this chapter. With each day of creation/destruction the candle is taken from its station, placed in the Earth bowl at the center of the church, and then extinguished. The seven candles remain extinguished until the Commitment at the end of the liturgy. The part of the Earth chorus, representing Earth crying out in pain, may be said or sung by a person or group located in the background.*

Leader        Sin not only violates our human community with God and each other, it also violates the community of all creation. Knowing that we are at one time or another complicit in this, we, as community in this place, acknowledge our failings and actively seek restored wholeness through God's re-creative work and promises in Jesus Christ.

### Station 1: Crystals Reflecting Light

Leader        On the first day of creation
You split the darkness and created light.

All        *On the first day of destruction
we split the atom, exploded nuclear devices,
and created a black mist of darkness/death.*

Earth chorus    Song: "I Groaned" (p. 177)

I groaned,
I quaked, I called, I groaned.

### Station 2: Feathers from the Sky

Leader        On the second day of creation
You created sky
filled with clouds, stars, and fresh air.

All        *On the second day of destruction
we began burning fossil fuels,
pumping fumes into the sky,
and created pollution.*

Earth chorus    I groaned,
I quaked, I called, I groaned.

## Station 3: Soil, Earth Vegetation, and Seeds

Leader       On the third day of creation
You gathered together the waters
revealing Earth, the source of rich vegetation,
forests, streams, and seeds for new life.

All       *On the third day of destruction*
*we began to strip the land,*
*creating barren salt plains with no life to grow;*
*then we began to woodchip and burn the forests,*
*removing over half Earth's vegetation*
*in less than a human lifetime.*

Earth chorus    I groaned,
I quaked, I called, I groaned.

## Station 4: Sun, Moon, and Seasons

Leader       On the fourth day of creation
You created the sun and the moon
and differentiated the day, the night, and the seasons.

All       *On the fourth day of destruction*
*we threw aerosols up into the sky,*
*ripping apart the protective ozone above,*
*and changing sunlight from friend to foe.*

Earth chorus    I groaned,
I quaked, I called, I groaned.

## Station 5: Birds and Sea Life

Leader       On the fifth day of creation
You called the sea and air to bring forth life
of many kinds for the wonder and delight of all.

All       *On the fifth day of destruction*
*we created DDT, killing the fish of the seas*
*and destroying the unborn birds of the air.*

Earth chorus    I groaned,
I quaked, I called, I groaned.

### Station 6: Animals Made from Clay

| | |
|---|---|
| Leader | On the sixth day of creation<br>You watched as the creatures of the land emerged,<br>crawling, leaping, and playing games of life. |
| All | *On the sixth day of destruction*<br>*we looked away as multitudes of species*<br>*disappeared through our destruction of habitations.* |
| Earth chorus | I groaned,<br>I quaked, I called, I groaned. |

### Station 7: Rest and Celebration

| | |
|---|---|
| Leader | On the seventh day of creation<br>you gave creation the blessing of rest<br>to celebrate and sustain all life. |
| All | *On the seventh day of destruction*<br>*we created the relentless drive for progress,*<br>*exploiting all life to increase profit.* |
| Earth chorus | I groaned,<br>I quaked, I called, I groaned. |

## Absolution

| | |
|---|---|
| Leader | Let us ask Christ for forgiveness for these days of destruction |
| All | *God, our Creator, forgive us for our crimes against creation,*<br>*our days of destruction on Earth;*<br>*and give us the courage in Christ*<br>*to work with Earth to bring healing and peace.* |
| Leader | Christ, our cosmic and risen companion,<br>forgives you all your wrongs against creation,<br>and fills you with the Spirit of the Creator,<br>so that you may learn to work together with Earth<br>to renew our corner of creation.<br>In the name of the Creator, Christ, and the Spirit. |
| All | *Amen.* |

**Song:** "Mother Earth, Our Mother Birthing" (p. 168)

**Prayers for the Day**

Lord's Prayer

## The Eucharist

| | |
|---|---|
| Leader | The Creator be with you. |
| All | *And also with you.* |
| Leader | Lift up your hearts. |
| All | *We lift them up to God.* |
| Leader | Let us celebrate with God. |
| All | *And celebrate with all creation.* |
| Leader | It is good that we should celebrate today, |

Leader    It is good that we should celebrate today,
celebrate with God, the Creator,
who saw all that God had made and cried,
"Good. Very Good! Wonderful."
It is good that we should celebrate today,
celebrate with all creation,
with the deserts, the trees, sky, and the seas,
as we thank God for the blessings and beauty of Earth.
It is especially good to celebrate today,
celebrate the presence of the Creator,
playing amid the wonders of planet Earth:
mysterious in the elements of bread and wine,
close in the community of those who eat this meal
and incarnate in the human creature, Jesus Christ,
who, on the night in which he was betrayed, took bread,
and when he had given thanks, broke it,
and gave it to his disciples saying,
"Take. Eat. This is my body which is given for you."
In the same way he took the cup, after the meal,
gave thanks and gave it to them saying,
"Drink of it, all of you.
This cup is the new covenant in my blood,
which is shed for you for the forgiveness of sins.

> So do this as often as you drink it,
> in remembrance of me."
> And the peace of Christ be with you always.

### Agnus Dei

All        O Christ, Lamb of God, you take away the sin of the world;
               have mercy on us.
               O Christ, Lamb of God, you take away the sin of the world;
               have mercy on us.
               O Christ, Lamb of God, you take away the sin of the world;
               grant us your peace. Amen.

### Distribution

*Music may be played during distribution that links us with the songs, sounds, and wonders of creation.*

## The Thanksgiving

Leader       Let us thank Christ for this meal

All        *And let us thank our Creator for our blessings.*

Leader       We thank you, God, for connecting us to Christ
              through this meal.
              Connect us more closely with our creation,
              so that we may work with Earth
              to bring healing and peace.
              In Jesus' name,

All        *Amen.*

**Song:** "Song of Healing" (p. 166)

## Commitment

## Reading

**Reading 4**     Matthew 28:1–6

*This reading reveals that not only did the disciples celebrate Christ's resurrection, but that Earth also responded with the energy and excitement of a "great earthquake." The seven people who extinguished the candles in the Earth Bowl now light them again and return them, at the appropriate points in the Commitment that follows, to their place in front of the seven symbols stationed around the church.*

Leader        On the first day of resurrection, Earth quaked
                      and celebrated with a bright light in the tomb.

All            *On this day we celebrate the light,*
                      *and promise Earth we will strive to remove*
                      *all nuclear darkness and death.*

Leader        On the first day of resurrection, Earth quaked
                      and an angel descended from sky.

All            *On this day we celebrate sky,*
                      *and promise Earth we will finds new ways*
                      *to keep our atmosphere fresh and clean.*

Leader        On the first day of resurrection, Earth quaked
                      and a stone rolled back to reveal a cave.

All            *We celebrate our rocks, our soil, our caves,*
                      *and we promise Earth we will work*
                      *to save its soil from salt and its forests from destruction.*

Leader        On the first day of resurrection, Earth quaked
                      as the sun rose on a very new day.

All            *We celebrate our sun, our moon, and our seasons,*
                      *and we promise Earth to refrain from ripping*
                      *into the ozone layer and destroying life on Earth.*

Leader        On the first day of resurrection, Earth quaked
                      and tidal waves swept across the seas.

All            *We celebrate our seas with all their glistening life,*
                      *and we promise Earth not to deposit more toxins*
                      *that kill the creatures of the ocean.*

Leader        On the first day of resurrection, Earth quaked
                      and all life on Earth felt the rumble of Christ rising.

All            *We celebrate all life that emerges from Earth,*
                      *and we promise Earth that we will work*
                      *to save all threatened species, including humans.*

| | |
|---|---|
| Leader | On every day of resurrection, Earth quakes somewhere reminding us to celebrate and sustain life. |
| *All* | *We celebrate with all creation,*<br>*and we promise Earth to hold life sacred*<br>*and find ways that sustain all forms of life.* |
| Earth chorus | WONDERFUL!<br>This Earth is wonder-full!<br>God's chosen place!<br>A soul in space!<br>Alive! Alive! Alive!<br>And wonder-full!<br>WONDERFUL! |

## Blessing

| | |
|---|---|
| Leader | May the sand beneath connect your feet to Earth;<br>may flowers in bloom connect your senses to Earth;<br>may butterflies in flight connect your soul to Earth;<br>and may God, the Creator,<br>and Christ, the Cosmic One,<br>and the Spirit, the Sustainer,<br>bless you and connect your spirit to Earth. |
| *All* | *Amen.* |

**Song:** "Song of Sky" (p. 150)

## Acknowledgments

The *Song of Earth* liturgy was created as a joint venture between Dr. Norman Habel and the Committee for Social Justice of the South Australian Council of Churches under the leadership of Rev. Vicki Waller. Contributors to the text and form of the liturgy include Karen Bass, Ros Poke, Colin Cargill, Tony Cox, Brian Robbins, and Nardia Symonds.

The liturgy was first celebrated as an ecumenical event at St. Stephen's Lutheran Church, Adelaide, in May 2001, as the first in a worship series celebrating the Season of Creation.

All Bible translations are by Dr. Norman Habel.

# THREE

# SONG OF SKY

**Earth says:
"I am stardust
and to stardust I shall return."**

## SETTING

This liturgy, based on Psalm 19, celebrates sky. In this celebration we are invited to listen to the word of God that sky speaks to us, to connect with the re-creating presence of God in sky and air, and to praise God for Earth, a piece of animated stardust from God's sky.

The point of departure for this celebration is Psalm 19, a psalm that invites us not only to gaze into the heavens but also to listen to sky. Sky is filled with God's glory, the visible presence of God; the sun and moon and stars testify to God's glory, and speak God's word to us. Sky reveals God's presence, power, and message to Earth. (For a discussion of God's glory see the reflection in the *Song of Sanctuary* liturgy, p. 27.)

A special feature of this liturgy is the way it integrates rich traditions from Native American peoples. The use of prayer sticks is designed to link us with the ground. The feather attached to the stick blows in the wind that carries the prayer to God and connects us with sky. The wind returns as the life-giving breath from God, who fills and renews all creation.

This liturgy was developed by a worshiping community in Oshkosh, Wisconsin. This community has found that Native American symbols can be powerful vehicles for helping Christian worshipers reconnect with God's creation.

The worship space may be arranged with a large bowl, filled with soil — the Earth bowl — at the center. In the direction of the four compass points — magnetic west, north, east, south — colored ropes, ribbons, or cloth are stretched from the bowl to the perimeter of the space. The colors used by many Native Americans to represent the four directions are

west — blue or black;
north — white;
east — red;
south — yellow.

Feathered sticks, at least one for each participant, are placed in four baskets at the perimeter end of each rope, ribbon, or cloth.[1]

## TEXT AND REFLECTION

### The Text

The translation that follows is based on the NRSV translation of Psalm 19, but has been modified by Norman Habel to make the language inclusive. The translation also uses YHWH, the sacred name of God. When the psalm is read aloud, this name can be read as *Adonai*, as Jewish readers would say it, or as "Lord" (the English translation of the Greek word *Adonai*), or it can be pronounced "Yahweh." The technical term "Torah" is also included to highlight its significance. This term is rendered either as "law" or "teaching," but in fact includes both meanings and refers specifically to the revelation of God to Moses.

### *Psalm 19: A Psalm of David*

*The heavens are telling the glory of God;*
*and sky proclaims God's handiwork.*
*Day to day pours forth speech,*
*and night to night declares knowledge.*
*There is no speech, nor are there words;*
*their voice is not heard;*
*yet their voice goes out through all Earth,*
*and their words to the end of the world.*

*In sky God has set a tent for the sun,*
*which comes out like a bridegroom from his wedding canopy,*
*and like a strong man runs his course with joy.*
*Its rising is from the end of the heavens,*
*and its circuit to the end of them;*
*and nothing is hid from its heat.*

---

1. Directions for preparation of the feather sticks are included on p. 66.

*The Torah of YHWH is perfect, reviving the soul;*
*the decrees of YHWH are sure, making wise the simple;*
*the precepts of YHWH are right, rejoicing the heart;*
*the commandment of YHWH is clear, enlightening the eyes;*
*the fear of YHWH is pure, enduring forever;*
*the ordinances of YHWH are true and righteous altogether.*
*More to be desired are they than fine gold;*
*sweeter also than honey, and drippings of the honeycomb.*

*Moreover by them is your servant warned;*
*in keeping them there is great reward.*
*But who can detect their errors?*
*Clear me from hidden faults.*
*Keep back your servant also from insolent thoughts,*
*do not let them have dominion over me.*
*Then I shall be blameless,*
*and innocent of great transgression.*

*Let the words of my mouth and the meditation of my heart*
*be acceptable to you, O YHWH, my rock and my redeemer.*

## Reflection, by William Urbrock

### Past Readings

Many scholars have questioned the unity of Psalm 19, suggesting that it was composed originally as two separate psalms: one celebrated the glory of God in the natural world (Psalm 19:1–6); the other was a meditation on God's special gift of Torah (law/teaching) to Israel (Psalm 19:7–14). Some scholars have suggested that Psalm 19:1–6 reflects an Israelite adaptation of a hymn to the sun from Canaan or elsewhere in the ancient Near East.

A traditional Jewish reading of the psalm would emphasize joy and celebration in the Torah of Moses, the books of Genesis, Exodus, Leviticus, Numbers, and Deuteronomy. After all, the psalm praises Torah as that which "revives the soul, makes wise the simple, rejoices the heart, and enlightens the eyes," and which is worth more than the finest gold.

A traditional Christian reading might focus on the penitential words at the close of the psalm, which emphasize the difficulty any human being has of keeping Torah, since "hidden faults" and "insolent thoughts" are always at hand. Hence, the closing verses are heard as a prayer for grace and forgiveness. In connection with Psalm 19:1–6, Christian theologians also have discussed the question of "natural revelation," how God is revealed to all peoples through nature or creation, as Paul suggests in Romans 1:20.

The final verse of Psalm 19 is familiar to many Christians as a prayer recited by pastors just before beginning a sermon. In addition, portions of the psalm have been popularized in Joseph Haydn's beloved oratorio *The Creation*. In his oratorio, after sun and moon and stars have been set in their places on the fourth day of creation, the archangel Uriel sings a recitative that includes the lines from Psalm 19 about the sun rising in splendor, rejoicing like a bridegroom, and preparing to run a race like a hero. Immediately, the heavenly choir responds by singing a magnificent chorus based on the opening words of the psalm: "The heavens are telling the glory of God, and sky proclaims God's handiwork."

### Reading the Text Again

What does it mean for sky to be telling the glory of God?

When read as a unified composition, Psalm 19 presents striking, side-by-side pictures of the divine word, almost like a triptych — an icon in three panels. The central panel (Psalm 19:7–10) portrays YHWH's particular revelation to Israel in the Torah of Moses. A series of synonyms (Torah meaning teaching, decrees, precepts, commandments, and ordinances) — similar to the eight repeated synonyms in the great Torah Psalm 119 — calls attention to the life-reviving, wisdom-imparting, heart-rejoicing, and enlightening qualities of the teaching YHWH revealed to Moses. As this Torah was given specifically to Israel, Israel's special name for God, YHWH, is prominent in this panel.

Flanking this picture of YHWH's Torah-word to Israel are two other panels. Like the side panels that open out into a triptych, these panels literally open out to show how God's word addresses and embraces everyone, even those to whom the Torah was not given. The first panel (Psalm 19:1–6) celebrates how the word of God communicates to all people everywhere, whatever their native tongue, through sky, through the regular alternation of day and night, and through the splendor of the sun.

In the final panel (Psalm 19:11–14), the psalmist, speaking as a "servant," asks that the rock and redeemer keep the speaker in the psalm from error and transgression. Then the psalmist concludes with the daring request that the speaker's words and meditation (evidently, including the words of this psalm itself!) "be acceptable," perhaps as a sort of substitute for an "acceptable" sacrifice offered at the Jerusalem Temple. How surprised the psalmist might be to discover that this psalm has been accepted by millions of believers as the word of God!

We can read Psalm 19 as a witness to the word of God active on three levels throughout the entire universe as we know and experience it today. First, the divine word speaks to all people worldwide through the proclamation of sky and the voices of the cosmos (Psalm 19:1–6). The cosmos is the theater of God's glory, the stage for God's self-revelation; its very structures speak of the all-encompassing ordinances of God. Next, the divine word addresses Israel through the sacred name YHWH and the Torah of Moses (Psalm 19:7–10). Finally, the divine word speaks in the heart and through the lips of every individual who faithfully meditates on and responds to the divine word conveyed by sky or by Torah.

## Sky Proclaims God's Glory

Two dominating icons of sky in our age are the film images of the atomic mushroom cloud and the television images of the first humans to orbit Earth, walk in space, and step foot on the moon.

The first icon reminds us powerfully of all the ways that we have abused sky: we have polluted the air, blackened the atmosphere, created acid rain, and spread atomic radiation. The exploding mushroom cloud of destruction — on a scale hardly imaginable to people of previous generations — almost silences sky's proclamation of God's glory and brings death to Earth and its inhabitants from above. The atomic cloud also reminds us of the accidental disaster at Chernobyl, the effects of which are yet to be played out completely. If we were to listen to the proclamation of sky today, would we not hear sky crying out in protest against our abuse? Might not the prayer for humility and for innocence from "great transgression" in Psalm 19:13 include a confession of our sins against sky and a resolve to change our ways?

The second set of images reminds us of how, in recent decades, sky has received humans and how the works of humanity have been thrust into its midst in ways only dreamed of in centuries past. Modern science has revealed to us a universe on a breathtakingly vast scale of time and space. Modern technology has enabled us to enter the nearer reaches of sky. Our telecommunications satellites now join the visible stars in sky above and around our world. Our rockets probe previously unknown reaches of space. Our space cameras send back pictures of distant planets. Our telescopes and listening devices probe sky for evidence of events that happened billions of years ago.

How amazing to realize that we are made of the same stuff as the stars and moon! Our planet is a fragile ball of stardust! How humbling to realize that we are intimately interconnected with sky and are in many ways dependent upon it for life and survival. As we learn more about the evolution of our universe and become more consciously "at home" in our surrounding sky — through whose vast expanse we travel and explore — we are invited to rejoice like the sun in Psalm 19. We are invited to delight in our discoveries. We also are challenged to be ever more alert to the messages of the heavens and sky, as they speak to us of the God who contains and creatively empowers and renews this vast universe.

## Preparing for Worship

As we prepare for worship, we are invited to listen to sky and the other voices in the cosmos and hear their proclamation of God's glory and life-giving creativity. God's word spoken through sky invites our faithful response; God addresses us through sky and the cosmos, through sacred Scriptures, or through the words and witness of human "servants" of God. We are mindful of our part in polluting our atmosphere and our responsibility as "servants" of God for keeping sky pure. We are mindful, too, of our privilege of living in and under sky, on our one Earth that whirls around one sun in one galaxy among the myriads of planets, moons, and stars in the universe. In the Christian Gospels, voices from sky celebrated Jesus' birth (Luke 2:13–14) and bore witness to Jesus' divine mission on the occasion of Jesus' baptism (Mark 1:9–11); a sky cloud received Jesus when he was lifted up after his farewell blessing (Luke 24:50–51 and Acts 1:8–10).

# LITURGY: SONG OF SKY

## Processional

*During the opening hymn a group of children may enter with ribbon banners, prayer flags, kites on poles, or other symbols they wave above the assembly to praise sky and the God of sky.*

**Song:** "Song of Sky" (p. 150)

## Invitation to Worship

| | |
|---|---|
| Leader | Come, enter into this sacred time and space and tell of the goodness of God. |
| All | *We join sky and all creation in proclaiming God's glory.* |
| Leader | Come to fill the universe with praise for the wonder of the Holy One's handiwork. Come to breathe in the Spirit and breathe out justice. |
| All | *We join sky and all creation in receiving God's life-reviving word and spirit.* |
| Leader | Come to offer thanks, to confess sin, and to remember — to re-member ourselves as the Body of Christ, that we might cooperate with all creation in serving God. |
| All | *We join sky and all creation in offering ourselves with joy for God's service.* |

## Confession

| | |
|---|---|
| Leader | For the gifts of sky and air, for your very breath of life, we give thanks to you, O God. We praise you for stars dancing in the cosmos, clouds floating in the heavens, and winds harboring soft breezes. We praise you for birds flying above Earth, for insects taking to wing, and for all that moves and changes at the wind's beckoning. How wonderful and mysterious are your gifts of sky and wind and breath! |
| | We confess, O God, that we have not always cared well for your creation. We have not always protected and justly used the gifts of creation: |

Through arrogance, greed, and ignorance, we have contaminated sky, hidden stars from our sight, choked the winds with toxins.

By our abuse of creation by contaminating the very air we breathe, we have caused suffering and death for Earth, for ourselves, and for all creatures dependent on Earth's atmosphere.

For our wrongs, O God, we ask forgiveness. Open our ears to the proclamation of your glory by the cosmos and sky, and turn our hearts that we might become better citizens of Earth and demonstrate more respect when we travel through sky.

Accept our actions of repentance. Let us breathe deeply of your redeeming breath, and enable us to reverence you in all that you have given us.

All        *O God, keep back your servants from insolent thoughts and great transgression. Make us wise by your decrees and enlighten us by your commandments. Let the words of our mouths and the meditation of our hearts be acceptable to you, O God, our rock and our redeemer. Amen.*

## Readings

**Reading 1**    Psalm 19

**Reading 2**    Isaiah 55:6–11

**Reading 3**    John 3:1–8

## *Sung Response: Alleluia.*

All        *Alleluia, Alleluia, Alleluia.*

## Reflection

**Litany** (based on a Native American tradition)

Leader      We greet you, O Spirit of God, as you come from the winds of the east. We acknowledge the home of the rising sun and the gifts of spring, birth, and babies. Fill us with the power of illumination and wisdom.

| | |
|---|---|
| All | *Spirit of God, our Creator, we offer you our thanksgiving.* |
| Leader | We greet you, O Spirit of God, as you come to us from the winds of the south. We acknowledge the home where the sun is at its highest and warmest. We acknowledge the gifts of summer, growth, and young people. Fill us with trust and the power to grow in new ways. |
| All | *Spirit of God, our Creator, we offer you our thanksgiving.* |
| Leader | We greet you, O Spirit of God, as you come to us from the winds of the west. We acknowledge the home where the day finds its fulfillment and the gifts of autumn and adulthood. Fill us with the power that comes from quiet reflection. |
| All | *Spirit of God, our Creator, we offer you our thanksgiving.* |
| Leader | We greet you, O Spirit of God, as you come to us from the winds of the north. We acknowledge the coldness of death and the gifts of winter and elderhood. Fill us with the power that comes from renewal and letting go. |
| All | *Spirit of God, our Creator, we offer you our thanksgiving.* |

## Rites for Connecting with Sky

*In this ritual each person is given a six-inch (15cm) length of straight tree branch or wooden stick. A feather is attached to the top of the branch or stick by wrapping yarn or string around it. The symbolism of the stick is that our prayers are grounded to Earth; the feather symbolizes how our prayers are carried by the wind of sky to the Creator.*

*The yarn may be red — the color of the tree of life in Sioux tradition. Additional yarn may be wrapped around the rest of the stick, in one or all of the four colors widely used among Native Americans: blue or black (for west), white (north), red (east), and yellow (south).*

*After the blessing, when the feathered branches have been distributed, everyone holds them during the prayers that follow. The sticks may then be "planted" in an Earth bowl filled with sand or soil in the sanctuary or somewhere outdoors to remain in place until nature reclaims them.*

*An alternative rite involves lengths of ribbon or unbleached linen distributed to each person. The ribbon is held during prayer time and bears the prayer of the person. The ribbons are then used as prayer ties (similar to Buddhist prayer flags) to let the prayer intentions be carried by the winds through sky to the Creator. The ribbons are tied to a tree or on a rope at the place of worship and left to fly in the wind until nature claims them.*

## The Blessing

Leader        Before us are feathered branches, symbols of growing life on Earth and of the winged creatures who soar aloft in air and sky. As trees are grounded to Earth, so are we; and our prayers arise from Earth. As feathers carry birds aloft in sky, so too the wings of our prayers carry praises aloft to our Creator. The colors of black, white, red, and yellow represent the four directions, west, north, east, and south, and the pathways to life.

All        *As we bless these feathered branches, we bless Earth and sky and declare them sacred. And we bless the Creator who gives us air and sky and the breath of life.*

Leader        We bless these feathered branches:
in the name of the Creator;
whose glory is declared by heavens,
and whose handiwork is proclaimed by sky;
in the name of the Christ,
whose praise resounded in the Skies
at his birth among us;
and in the name of the Spirit,
who, like the winds from the four directions,
blows the breath of renewing life for us and all creation.

All        *Amen! May sky be holy for us.*

## Sharing

*Everyone present receives a feathered branch.*

## Bidding Prayers

*The leader prays the bids, and the people gathered, holding their feathered branches, respond: May God's breath renew them!*

Leader        Birds, insects, all creatures that take to flight in air:

All        *May God's breath renew them!*

| | |
|---|---|
| Leader | People who fly through sky, airplane pilots, balloonists, researchers, and astronauts: |
| All | *May God's breath renew them!* |
| Leader | Company executives, politicians, and investors who choose pollution of the air for the sake of profits: |
| All | *May God's breath renew them!* |
| Leader | Those who work in polluted environments, coal miners, chemical plant workers, and others: |
| All | *May God's breath renew them!* |
| Leader | Those with emphysema, asthma, bronchitis, and other chronic lung diseases: |
| All | *May God's breath renew them!* |
| Leader | Those who fill their lives with stress and have forgotten how to breathe deeply: |
| All | *May God's breath renew them!* |
| Leader | Sky and air, polluted by the works of our hands; trees, rivers, lakes, and forest creatures suffering from acid rain: |
| All | *May God's breath renew them!* |
| Leader | Scientists, researchers, engineers, and all those who seek to befriend the air and wind as sources of energy: |
| All | *May God's breath renew them!* |
| Leader | All who promote and foster good winds of change: |
| All | *May God's breath renew them!* |
| Leader | Daydreamers, kite fliers, cloud watchers, star gazers, all who look at sky and cosmos with wonder and listen to their proclamation of God's glory: |
| All | *May God's breath renew them!* |

*Individual prayers may be offered aloud or silently. After the prayers are concluded, the feathered branches may be "planted" in the Earth bowl.*

*Each person may silently pray, taking three deep breaths and blowing through the feathers to God.*

**Song:** "Rise, Creator Spirit, Rise" (p. 180)

## The Eucharist

### Eucharistic Prayer

Leader    God of breath and life,
of star-swept sky and windswept shores,
God of gentle breezes, rushing winds, and fresh, clean air:
It is indeed right that we should celebrate you,
through whom, in whom, and from whom
sky and all creation draw life and breath.
Filled with wonder and delight,
we declare with sky and all creation:

All    *Holy, Holy, Holy Lord, God of power and might,*
*sky and Earth are full of your glory!*
*Hosanna in the highest!*
*Blessed is one who comes in the name of YHWH!*
*Hosanna in the highest!*

Leader    We remember your care for us, great God.
You are holy, wonderful, a God of manifold blessings.

All    *We remember Jesus the beloved one:*
*sky rang with angelic songs at his birth,*
*the Spirit and voices from sky proclaimed him*
*the chosen Son at his baptism,*
*sky received him after he gave his disciples a parting blessing.*

Leader    We remember how, on the night before he died, Jesus gathered with his friends for a meal of love:

[*Words of Institution*]

As Jesus once gathered with his friends, so Jesus gathers with us now, sharing his love, his truth, and the breath of his Spirit.

All    *In that same Spirit, Jesus invites us to breathe deeply of the mystery of life, to be at one with God and with all God has created.*

| | |
|---|---|
| Leader | Send the renewing breath of your Spirit upon our church, upon our families, friends, all people, and all creatures in Earth and sky. |
| All | *Teach us to value the gifts of your creation, and lead us to act with justice toward all people, all creatures and elements.* |

## Distribution

## Commitment

*Special prayers for the day, for sky, and for the crises of Earth and sky may be said; each prayer may be followed by a commitment.*

| | |
|---|---|
| Leader | Let us commit our lives to God and resolve to walk in greater harmony with Earth and all its creatures and to listen more closely to the voices of sky proclaiming the glory of God. |
| All | *Lord, today we greet your Spirit as you come to us on the winds of the west with the breath of power, courage, and transformation.* |
| | *We greet your Spirit as you come to us on the winds of the north with the breath of cleansing, healing, and stability.* |
| | *We greet your Spirit as you come to us on the winds of the east with the breath of new beginnings, enlightenment, and wisdom.* |
| | *We greet your Spirit as you come to us on the winds of the south with the breath of growth, abundance, and security.* |
| | *We choose this day to walk the pathways of peace and renewal beneath your sky.* |
| | *We pledge to work for an end to the polluting of the air and sky.* |
| | *We promise to listen more closely for the divine word that the sky proclaims to us, as day to day pours forth speech and night to night declares knowledge.* |

## Closing Blessing

Leader
May our eyes be blessed that we may see God's beauty in the star-swept sky;

may our ears be blessed that we may hear God calling us in the wind;

may our hearts be blessed that we may feel the love of God in the warmth of the sun.

May God, our Creator, Redeemer, and Sanctifier, bless us with each life-renewing breath we take!

All
*Amen!*

Leader
Go in peace to serve the God of Earth and sky!

All
*Thanks be to God!*

## Acknowledgements

This liturgy was written and arranged jointly by Joseph Blotz (student, University of Wisconsin Oshkosh), Kathryn Schreitmueller (pastor, Lutheran Campus Ministry, Oshkosh, Wisconsin), William J. Urbrock (professor of Religious Studies, University of Wisconsin Oshkosh), and Linda A. Zahorik (parish liturgist, St. Peter's Catholic Community, Oshkosh, Wisconsin).

# FOUR

# SONG OF WATERS

**Earth says:**
**"I am a living planet,**
**robed in green and blue water and glistening."**

## SETTING

The *Song of Waters* liturgy focuses on water as the source of life, a means of new life and a vehicle for healing, and was developed with the input of a number of people involved in an e-mail discussion group focused on ecotheology and the ecological crisis. Planet Earth is characterized by its water, an essential feature of its life-sustaining capacity. Astronauts have commented on the unique blueness of Earth, like a bright blue bauble suspended in the surrounding blackness of space. Psalm 104 is the key background text for *Song of Waters*. This psalm celebrates YHWH, the God of Waters, and in this psalm God controls, shares, celebrates, and plays in the waters.

The setting for this liturgy is the world of living waters. Water symbols may be used as appropriate in a worship place. The focal symbol is a large bowl of clear water, raised on a pedestal; it represents both the living waters from God, the waters of baptism, and the life-giving and healing waters arising from Earth. A long blue piece of fabric may be used to represent these living waters flowing from the bowl into, through, and around the worshiping community. Large glass jugs filled with water may be carried in and used to fill the bowl during an opening procession. The sound of the water emphasizes these are living, flowing streams from God and Earth. Leaves representing the healing leaves from the tree of life in Revelation 22:1–2 may be floated on the top of the water in the bowl and be strewn along the blue fabric stream. The fabric may also be adorned with flowers or some other symbol of celebration.

Four smaller bowls are located at stations nearby. Water may be taken from the large bowl and poured into these bowls. During the confession, pollutants are added to these smaller bowls to symbolize our treatment of Earth's waters. In a procession at the end of the service these smaller bowls are taken outside and the polluted water poured into the ground for cleansing. Especially important for this ground is the fate of Earth's waters and rain forests; the vitality of both is crucial to the future of life on this planet, and for the life of Earth. We also need to be aware that we have polluted and defiled the life-giving waters of Earth. In Jesus, the water of life, we have the power to discover again the life-breath, the living spirit of God that renews all dimensions of life and brings healing to our planet.

Our originating element is water; it is a fitting symbol for our God who gives us life, brings us healing through water, and sustains our life-breath. In Genesis, we are fashioned from clay; that clay is predominantly water. In death, we stop breathing air, and we dry out. Removing our water or access to air is a sure killer. And living Earth is no exception: our planet sustains life because it has water and oxygen-filled air. Without both, it becomes a dead planet, devoid of diverse, flourishing, bountiful living things.

## TEXTS AND REFLECTION

### Texts

In this study we explore briefly the biblical background and environmental context of the liturgy. This reflection is intended to help us celebrate the mystery of the waters in our world, revere this wondrous planet that is so dependent on water, and commit ourselves to work with Earth in restoring its waters.

Three texts support the key focuses in this liturgy. Norman Habel's translation of Psalm 104, included below, emphasizes how God is involved in providing and celebrating water as a life-giving component of this planet. The Epistle reading from Romans 6 focuses on water as the vehicle God uses to bring new life through baptism. The Gospel reading from John 9 portrays Jesus directing the blind man to wash in the waters of the pool of Siloam for healing. The waters celebrated in these texts are both life-giving and healing waters.

## Psalm 104

Bless YHWH, O my soul.
O YHWH my God, you are very great.
You are clothed with honor and majesty,
wrapped in light as in a garment.
You stretch out the sky like a tent;
you set the beams of your upper rooms in the waters;
you make the clouds your chariots;
you ride on the wings of the wind,
and make the winds your messengers,
fire and flame your ministers.
You set Earth on its foundations,
so that Earth will never be shaken.
You cover Earth with the deep as with a cloak;
waters stand above the mountains.
At your rebuke they flee;
your thunderous voice sends them running. . . .
You make springs gush forth from the valleys;
they flow between the hills,
giving drink to all wild animals;
the wild asses quench their thirst;
by the streams the birds of the air have their habitation;
they sing among the branches.
From your upper rooms you water the mountains;
Earth is satisfied with the fruit of your work.
You cause the grass to grow for the cattle,
and plants for people to use,
to bring forth food from Earth:
wine to gladden the human heart,
oil to make the face shine,
and bread to strengthen the human heart.
The trees of YHWH are watered abundantly,
the cedars of Lebanon that God planted. . . .

O YHWH, how manifold are your works!
Through Wisdom you made them all.
Earth is full of your creatures.
There — sea, great and wide;

*there — creeping things innumerable;*
*Living things — the small with the great.*
*There go ships —*
*and Leviathan you formed to play with. . . .*

*You hide your face, they panic;*
*when you take away your breath/spirit they die.*
*When you send forth your breath/spirit they are created;*
*and you renew the face of the ground.*
*May the glory of YHWH be forever;*
*may YHWH celebrate YHWH's creations,*
*looking on Earth so that Earth trembles,*
*touching the mountains so that they smoke.*

## Reflection, by Norman Habel

### Past Readings

Psalm 104 has often been seen as a poetic version of Genesis 1, a variation of the story of creation. Reading the psalm this way, we tend to watch God performing mighty acts of creation — albeit in colorful language — in the past and in the present. The psalm's creative activity is more "hands on" than the "word-acts" of Genesis 1, where God speaks and Earth acts. In this respect the psalm is more evocative of Genesis 2, where God is portrayed as a gardener or landscape artist and as a clay-sculptor, breathing life into creatures fashioned from soil mixed with water.

Many parts of the cosmos listed in Genesis 1 are, in fact, mentioned in Psalm 104: light, sky, Earth, waters, plant life, animal and bird life, sea, and sun.

If, however, we read the text again without making a mental or conscious link with Genesis 1, we discover that at no point in the psalm does an originating act of creation take place. In Psalm 104, God uses what is already there to establish a home, transport, playmates, and to set limits on sea. The psalm is about God in the midst of our creation here and now — especially among the waters. In Psalm 104, waters are a central domain of the wild, of creation unspoiled by human hands.

What does it mean that God is so closely connected with creation — and especially waters?

### Reading the Text Again

Psalm 104 begins with a description of God stretching out sky as a tent, like the tabernacle of old: the tent sanctuary where God once appeared. God also builds upper rooms, but not in some distant heaven. In Psalm 104 — as the Hebrew original makes clear — the upper rooms are above Earth, "in the waters" of sky. When God is in God's tent home, God is actively at work in sky, the water-world above Earth (Psalm 104:2–3).

And when God appears in sky, what form does God take? A rain cloud! God flies across sky in the rain clouds; God's transport appears as a massive chariot accompanied by winds as messengers announcing God's coming to rain on Earth. The God in Psalm 104 is depicted like an ancient storm god: God is in the storm, riding on the wings of the wind, celebrating the showers and ultimately coming to baptize Earth with life-giving, healing waters (Psalm 104:3–4).

A second feature of this psalm, already implied in God's wild chariot ride across the sky, is the element of play. In describing Earth, the psalmist reminds us that Earth is firmly fixed on its foundations. As if to prove the point, the psalmist depicts God's cosmic playfulness. The deep, which in ancient times was believed to be a great mass of water below Earth in which Earth's foundations are fixed, is poured over Earth. The image is of God, like a child playing on the beach, tipping water over a sand castle. The psalmist describes God at play with serious intent: God tips the world upside down, up-ends the deep, and immerses Earth with the waters from the deep. God is baptizing Earth with the waters of the deep. Earth does not move. But the waters do! Then God thunders "Boo!" and the waters of the deep scramble to fall in line (Psalm 104:5–9).

God not only puts the deep in its place, God also turns on a system of springs, streams, and showers to water all life on Earth. God summons water from below and above, from low places in the ground and God's upper rooms in sky. The first are like deep reservoirs beneath the land; the second like massive water tanks on high. The result is that Earth is sated, completely satisfied with the water all life on Earth needs to flourish (Psalm 104:10–13). As a result God's wish for Earth comes true: Earth is fruitful, life multiplies, and Earth is teeming with life. Earth is a living planet, the wondrous blue-with-water-planet in God's cosmos.

The response to this blessing is a celebration of life as bounty. Earth flows with grain and wine and oil. Life is depicted as more than bread or the basics of survival. There is wine to make the human heart rejoice in celebration and oil to make the face shine with festive joy. The image is replete with excess: people can eat more than they need and make wine to drink for pleasure. Their bodies gleam with good living. In the ancient world, bodies were rubbed with oil to celebrate the good times when there was more than enough food, and the whole group — including the young and old, the most vulnerable in times when there is less than enough — is assured of survival.

However, God's bounty and blessing do not end with human beings. God also waters the garden where God planted great cedars. And God makes sure the creatures of the wild get fed each night (Psalm 104:14–23). In Psalm 104, God's loving kindness extends to all creation. God celebrates all creation and ensures there is enough for everyone to share.

Perhaps the boldest and most playful image of Psalm 104 appears in verses 24–26. After suggesting that God is a careful creator, using Wisdom like an ancient sage to guide and order everything in the cosmos, the psalmist invites us to take a closer look at the world of sea. There is something about sea that captures the human imagination. It was a mystery for ancient peoples, and there are still places in the deepest parts of oceans that humans know very little about, that are still sources of mystery, delight, surprise, and wonder. Sea's fascinating diversity of creeping life-forms can never be calculated. In the vast oceans of Earth, massive animals live together with, and collaborate with, minute organisms. Complementariness is a basic fact of life in sea.

If you take a closer look, suggests the psalmist, you can see Leviathan, a great sea monster feared by peoples of old. If you take an even closer look you can see God playing games with this creature in the ocean waves, like a swimmer hitching a ride into the deep with dolphins, a diver swimming near a whale, a human wrestling with a crocodile or tickling a giant shark. This is challenging play from a human perspective: a dangerous opportunity for pleasure! Whatever the image, although sea may be a place for humans to respect and fear, for God it is a place to play (Psalm 104:24–26). God respects human free will; perhaps this image underlines that God values the free will of all creation and respects and delights in the opportunities for potentially dangerous play with things that bite and kill. And perhaps there is a message here for us, too: the creatures of the wild are challenging — filled with danger and opportunity — and their right to playful life is to be respected and celebrated.

## Fertility, Serendipity, Moist Breath

Psalm 104 captures a sense of the presence of waters above, below, and across Earth. The waters, however, are not just "there" as tourist attractions. The presence of God permeates the waters. They are life-giving waters, waters that wash and cleanse, waters filled with a diversity of microscopic to macroscopic life, and the waters that baptize Earth into life in the beginning. This is not God creating a cosmos as is suggested by many readings of Genesis 1, but the God of fertility, active in all the ecosystems of life on Earth. And each of these is dependent on water — water from raging thunderstorms and tropical cyclones to silent trickling springs and dewy transpiration. Our planet is indeed a water-world, and Psalm 104 celebrates Earth's waters.

In a remarkable way this psalm anticipates our contemporary understanding of how water connects all life and fertility in the ecosystems of Earth. Psalm 104:29–30 declares that God's presence is essential to all life, and at the same time points us back to the waters that permeate the planet. In this psalm, the moist breath, wind, spirit of God is not a spiritual invasion from heaven, but the very moisture, oxygen, wind, life-breath that continuously creates life, facilitates fertility, and renews life. The moist breathing of God keeps Earth alive.

There is more to this psalm than images of God sustaining ecosystems. Wherever God is involved, it seems, there is a certain serendipity, a hint of divine humor, an element of active play. God rides on the winds of the wind bringing rain, tips the deep upside down to baptize Earth with life, provides wine and oil for celebrating life, plays with Leviathan and sea creatures in celebration of their challenges and the dangerous opportunities they represent.

And, just in case we do not quite recognize the celebrative playfulness of it all, the psalmist calls on YHWH to rejoice in all creation, to join us in celebration. Earth certainly does — and trembles with delight at the fireworks display God provides!

> May the glory of YHWH be forever;
> may YHWH celebrate YHWH's creations,
> looking on Earth so that Earth trembles,
> touching the mountains so that they smoke.
> (Psalm 104:31–32)

Liturgies

And perhaps the greatest mystery of all: God's glory and God's play are linked inextricably in Psalm 104.

## Defiling the Waters

We are now aware that, in our greed and folly, we have defiled, polluted, and poisoned many of the waters of Earth. Even life in the vast oceans is being killed at an alarming rate. Carl Safina, in his book *Song for the Blue Ocean*, outlines in detail how local fisherfolk are told to use cyanide as "medicine" to catch fish in the coral reef of the Philippines.[1] Louise Bodigans, also from the Philippines, gives us a personal report of what is happening today.

> The Philippines, like Planet Earth, has more water than land. Our deepest oceans are deeper than Mt. Everest is high. The beauty and diversity of life in the seas is an underwater paradise richer than anything on land. Alas, increasing numbers of people enjoy the wealth of the sea captured in fish tanks in homes, offices, and restaurants. Most aquarium fish come from the Philippines and Indonesia; more than half are harvested using the poison cyanide. Divers squirt cyanide into reefs to stun fish, killing smaller fish and coral in the process. Only one in ten captured fish survive. Two-thirds of the world's 1.5 million aquarium hobbyists live in the United States. They buy half of the aquarium fish and up to 80 percent of the coral traded in the world. The next largest importers are Germany and Japan. Maybe they bring joy to many people in these places. But the oceans have been robbed of their wealth. Our paradise is being poisoned.

## Preparing for Worship

Before the worship begins ask four people to read the words of Speakers 1 through 4. The Speakers need to be supplied with the "pollutants" they will add to the water during the liturgy.

As you prepare for worship, you are invited to view Earth as wet, wild, and wonderful, and as a place of celebration — for humans, for all life-forms and for our God. You are invited to connect with our God as the playful fertilizing presence that fills our planet.

---

1. Carl Safina, *Song for the Blue Ocean: Encounters along the World's Coasts and Beneath the Seas* (New York: Henry Holt, 1997).

# LITURGY: SONG OF WATERS

**Song:** "Song of Sky" (p. 150)

*During this song, a procession may take place in which members of the group enter carrying large water jugs, green branches, and flowers. They stand around a large water bowl raised on a pedestal. This water bowl is the focal symbol for the worship. During the invocation pour the water from the jugs into the bowl and scatter healing leaves from the branches on the water.*

*Alternatively, the bowl may be filled with water prior to beginning the liturgy. However, the sound of pouring water adds a powerful aural element to the liturgy.*

## Invocation

Leader       Creator, source of living waters,

All       *come, baptize our planet,*
      *make it wet with blessing.*

Leader       Christ, living water among us,

All       *come, heal us with water*
      *in body, mind, and heart.*

Leader       Spirit, bring waters on the wind,

All       *come blow through our lives*
      *and refresh our spirits each day.*

## Readings

**Reading 1**       Psalm 104:24–34

Reader       O YHWH, how manifold are your works!
      Through Wisdom you made them all.
      Earth is full of your creatures.
      There — sea, great and wide;
      there — creeping things innumerable;
      Living things — the small with the great.
      There go ships —
      and Leviathan you formed to play with. . . .

All       *Come, Creator, celebrate your creations with us!*

| | |
|---|---|
| Reader | All of them look to you, |
| | to give them food in due season. |
| | You give to them, they gather; |
| | you open your hand, they are satisfied with good. |
| | You hide your face, they panic; |
| | when you take away your breath/spirit they die. |
| | When you send forth your breath/spirit they are created; |
| | and you renew the face of the ground. |
| All | *Come, Creator, celebrate your creations with us!* |
| Reader | May the glory of YHWH be forever; |
| | may YHWH celebrate YHWH's creations, |
| | looking on Earth so that Earth trembles, |
| | touching the mountains so that they smoke. |
| | Let me sing to YHWH while I am alive; |
| | let me make music to my God while I am. |
| | May my thoughts delight YHWH. |
| | I, I will celebrate with YHWH! |
| All | *Come, Creator, celebrate your creations with us!* |
| Reader | This is the word of the Lord. |
| All | *Thanks be to God.* |

### Litany: Response to Psalm 104

*Divide the worship group into two sections: A and B.*

| | |
|---|---|
| Leader | Wise God of living waters, |
| | your presence fills sky and sea, |
| | from the highest mountain rain forest |
| | to the darkest ocean depth, |
| | you dwell within a wondrous world of water! |
| | Come, let us celebrate together! |
| Group A | Let us celebrate with God, |
| | and join the festival of waters. |
| Group B | Let us play and dance with God; |
| | let us sail and surf, splash and swim. |
| All | *Let all creation praise God's fountain fullness!* |

| | |
|---|---|
| Leader | Wise God of living waters, |
| | we see your mystery in the gathering clouds, |
| | we smell your fresh, new life in the salty ocean spray; |
| | we hear your laughter in the splashing waterfall; |
| | we touch your goodness in the cool, green grass; |
| | we taste your generosity in the wine and bread. |
| | Come let us celebrate the water of life! |
| | |
| Group B | Let us celebrate with God; |
| | let us honor all water life, great and small. |
| | |
| Group A | Let us celebrate with pelicans, whales, and crayfish, |
| | salmon, mollusks, sea gulls, and albatross. |
| | |
| All | *Let all creation praise God's fountain fullness!* |
| | |
| Leader | Wise God of living waters, |
| | you bathe all creation each new dawn |
| | in the cleansing mist of the morning. |
| | We feel your freshness in dew and snow; |
| | we taste your tears in the rain. |
| | Come, let us celebrate our moist planet! |
| | |
| Group A | Let us be baptized every day, |
| | and feel the cleansing waters of rebirth. |
| | |
| Group B | Let us breathe in the moist breath of God |
| | and sing together sea's salty song. |
| | |
| All | *Let all creation praise God's fountain fullness!* |

**Song:** "Song of Waters" (p. 154)

## Confession

*During the confession each of the small clear bowls will be used to symbolize one of the ways humans have polluted Earth's waters: in oceans, rivers, underground waters, and through the water in the air.*

*Prior to the group response, and after each call to confess, the leader draws water from the central bowl into a jug and pours the water into one of the small clear bowls. A member of the group then adds a pollutant to the bowl to symbolize how humans have polluted or defiled the living waters. These group members proclaim the cry at the end of the confession.*

*Some examples of pollutants you may use are: a red dye representing poisons; used car oil representing industrial pollution; detergents representing modern chemicals; salt representing salination; plastic and tin lids, small plastic bags, and detergent representing non-biodegradable solid wastes.*

Leader    Let us remember our life-and-death connection with water.

*The leader fills a jug with water from the large bowl and pours it back into the large bowl. The group response begins as the water is poured back into the bowl.*

All
*We are born of water.*
*Without water we die.*
*Our personal creation story begins in our mother's womb,*
*in a watery sac;*
*our personal salvation story begins with our baptism,*
*when we become God's children.*

Leader    Let us remember how water is sacred to life on Earth.

*The leader again fills a jug from the large bowl and pours it back into the bowl. The group response begins as the water is poured into the bowl.*

All
*We are baptized into life through water.*
*We celebrate water as a blessing from God.*
*We are part of a mysterious cycle of life linked by water.*

Leader    Let us confess how we have destroyed life in our waters with poisons.

*The leader again fills the jug from the larger bowl and then moves to the first small bowl and fills it with water. Speaker 1 moves from the group to the bowl and pours a bright dye representing poison into the bowl from a small bottle labeled "poison."*

All
*We have polluted our waters with poisonous chemicals and destroyed life.*

Speaker 1    Can you hear the waters weeping?

Leader    Let us confess how we have destroyed life in our waters with industrial wastes.

*The leader fills the jug from the larger bowl and then moves to a second small bowl and fills it with water. Speaker 2 moves from the group to the bowl and pours used car oil into the bowl from a small bottle labeled "industrial waste."*

| | |
|---|---|
| All | We have flushed industrial waste into our oceans and rivers and destroyed life. |
| Speakers 1–2 | Can you hear the waters weeping? |
| Leader | Let us confess how we have destroyed life in our waters through agricultural practices that pollute groundwater. |

*Salination is a problem in Australia; in other contexts there may be another form of pollution such as herbicide use that may be more appropriate to cite.*

*The leader fills the jug from the larger bowl and then moves to the third small bowl and fills it with water. Speaker 3 moves from the group to the bowl and pours coarse salt into the bowl from a small dish labeled "salt" or "herbicide."*

| | |
|---|---|
| All | We have caused the groundwaters of our land<br>to become poisoned<br>and destroyed life. |
| Speakers 1–3 | Can you hear the waters weeping? |
| Leader | Let us confess how we have destroyed life in our waters with non-biodegradable human wastes. |

*The leader fills the jug from the larger bowl and then moves to a fourth smaller bowl and fills it with water. Speaker 4 moves from the group to the bowl and pours plastic and tin lids and small plastic bags and detergent from a bowl labeled "non-biodegradable human waste."*

| | |
|---|---|
| All | We have tipped non-biodegradable human wastes<br>into our waters<br>and destroyed life. |
| Speakers 1–4 | Can you hear the waters weeping? |
| All | Forgive us for our sins against our Creator and our Earth.<br>Forgive us for the life we have destroyed.<br>Give us Wisdom to purify Earth's waters. |

| Leader | In the name of our Creator God, |
|---|---|
| | and our God-human savior, Jesus Christ, |
| | I assure you |
| | that your sins against your Creator are forgiven. |
| | Creation is still groaning, suffering |
| | under the weight of our carelessness, |
| | our thoughtlessness — |
| | the things we have done |
| | and have not done — |
| | and pleads with us all to work with Earth, |
| | together with God, God's Spirit, |
| | and with God's Wisdom, Jesus Christ, |
| | to heal and purify Earth's living waters. |
| | May the three-person God: Creator, Wisdom, and Spirit, |
| | work in you and through you to restore the living waters. |
| | In the name of God, Jesus Christ, and the God-Spirit. |
| | Amen. |

## Readings

| **Reading 2** | Romans 6:1–4 |
|---|---|
| Leader | This is the word of our God. |
| *All* | *Thanks be to you, O Christ.* |
| **Reading 3** | John 9:1–11 |
| Leader | This is the Gospel of our God. |
| *All* | *Praise be to you, O Christ.* |

**Song:** "Song of Healing" (p. 166)

## Reflection

*Select from the reflections prepared for this liturgy or use your own reflection.*

## The Creed

*This version of the Creed picks up themes apparent in this liturgy. Groups may use one of the traditional church creeds if preferred.*

All         *We believe in God who creates all things,*
*who embraces all things, who celebrates all things,*
*who is present in every part of the fabric of creation.*
*We believe in God as the source of all life,*
*who baptizes this planet with living water,*
*who heals all the wounds of Earth.*
*We believe in the book of Earth, the book of life unfolding,*
*the book revealing the mysteries of God's wisdom.*
*We believe in Jesus Christ*
*as the revelation and Wisdom of God,*
*joining the web of life as human flesh,*
*Jesus is the love of God immersed in the cosmos.*
*We believe in an Earth community,*
*a community where lives of all creatures are interconnected.*
*We believe in Life forever,*
*empowered by the breath of the Spirit of God,*
*connected with our cosmic Christ*
*and celebrated by all creation.*

**Song:** "Mother Earth, Our Mother Birthing" (p. 168)

**Prayers**

*If the prayers focus on water, the following response may be said after each petition.*

Leader       God of living waters,

All         *Heal our planet's living waters.*

*Lord's Prayer*

**Eucharist**

Leader       The Creator be with you.

All         *And also with you.*

Leader       Lift up your hearts.

All         *We lift them up to God.*

Leader       Let us celebrate with God.

All         *Let us celebrate with all creation.*

Leader        It is good that we should celebrate today with the God of living waters, who has baptized this planet with blessings and clothed it with life. It is good that we celebrate with the Creator who celebrates in all God's creations, from the most minute life-forms to great and wondrous whales.

It is also good to celebrate the Spirit, the moist breath of God that renews the face of Earth.

But we celebrate especially that God became a living thing on this planet, joined the web of life, and became flesh in Jesus Christ. As part of this planet, Christ suffered for us and continues to suffer with creation, bringing healing in body and spirit to all who come to his table.

## Words of Institution

*The worship group may use any form they choose.*

## Invitation

*If the bowl of living waters is not conveniently located, the leader should fill a jug with water from the bowl and fill a smaller clear bowl placed on a pedestal located in front of the altar prior to the invitation to the Eucharist. This is the bowl used in the healing rite linked to the Eucharist. As necessary, the leader should change the description of the process to suit the particular practices and arrangement of facilities chosen to facilitate the distribution and the healing rite for those who choose to be blessed at the altar.*

Leader        Come to the meal prepared by Jesus Christ and our Creator.

In preparation for receiving the healing power of Christ's body and blood in the Sacrament, as you walk past the bowl of living waters, you may choose to dip your fingers in the water to remember your baptism and to connect your-self symbolically with the living waters from God. Those who wish a special healing through water and the lay-ing on of hands are invited to remain at the altar after receiving the cup.

Come, for all things are now ready.

### Agnus Dei

All       *O Christ, Lamb of God, you take away the sin of the world;*
             *have mercy on us.*
             *O Christ, Lamb of God, you take away the sin of the world;*
             *have mercy on us.*
             *O Christ, Lamb of God, you take away the sin of the world;*
             *grant us your peace. Amen.*

### Distribution

*After receiving the cup, those who remain at the altar for a healing through water and the laying on of hands receive a blessing from the leader or a group member designated to do so. The leader or group member should sprinkle water on the individual, lay on hands, and say:*

Leader       May Christ, the Living Water of God,
             flow through your body and your soul
             to bring you healing.

*When the Eucharist is ended and all who desire it have received a healing touch, the leader may bless the whole gathering with these words:*

Leader       May the living waters of your baptism continue to be active in your life, renewing you daily, and strengthening your work as the healing hands of our healer, Jesus Christ, on Earth. As you hear the sounds of water, wash and refresh yourself, and drink water every day, may you be reminded of your baptism and the active presence of the God of living waters in your life. In the name of God the Creator, Jesus the Wisdom of creation, and the Spirit, who keeps us holy and in close relationship with our God. Amen.

**Song:** "Song of the Wild" (p. 171)

### Thanksgiving

Leader       Let us thank Jesus Christ for this healing meal.
             Let us thank our Creator for the blessing of water.

All       *We thank you God for connecting us with creation,*
             *for bringing us healing through Christ's body and blood,*

*and for imparting new life through the moist breath*
*of the Spirit that fills our bodies.*
*In Jesus' name. Amen.*

## Renewal

Leader    As we leave, let us commit ourselves to working with Jesus and with creation, to heal creation, sustain Earth, and restore its waters to their pristine purity.

*Before the following words are spoken, the bowls of polluted water are sealed in a container marked "water purification" and later removed to the appropriate facilities.*

Leader    To return these waters we have polluted to their pristine state, we promise to use our technical expertise to remove the impurities and deal with these products of our human lifestyle in ways that do not harm Earth, Earth's waters, or other beings in creation.

We ask God to guide us in developing strategies for purifying what we have contaminated.

We ask God to give us the wisdom to refuse to use these contaminants for the sake of Earth, Earth's waters, and all creation.

We commit ourselves to restoring Earth,
and working toward keeping
our rivers clean from chemicals,
our oceans free from industrial waste,
our land free from excessive salt and herbicides,
our waterways free from household rubbish,
and our atmosphere free from greenhouse gases.

*All*    *Amen.*

We promise to work toward healing Earth's waters, with the help of God the Creator, Jesus, the Wisdom and healer of creation, and God's Spirit, who keeps us strong in the faith and in close relationship with our God. Amen.

Leader    May Christ give you the strength, the wisdom, and the courage to work toward justice for Earth, the planet God has made our home and blessed with living waters. Amen.

## Blessing

*Carrying one of the smaller water bowls placed at the altar prior to the Eucharist, the leader fills the smaller bowl with water from the bowl of living waters and moves through the gathering, dipping a small branch into the water and sprinkling the heads of the worshipers while repeating the following blessing. Speakers 1–4 may also sprinkle the group with water from the bowls filled from the bowl of living waters.*

Leader    May the moist breath of God heal this Earth and Earth's living waters. May the waters of life flow through your veins, and may the water of your baptism keep you in Jesus Christ, the healer of all creation. Amen.

**Song:** "Rise, Creator Spirit, Rise" (p. 180)

## Acknowledgments

*Song of Waters* is largely a collation of materials prepared by members of an ecotheology e-mail topica group in Australia and New Zealand. Special mention is made of contributions by Robert Bos, Pauline Coll, Nancy Victorin Vangerud, and Norman Habel.

# FIVE

# SONG OF SOPHIA

**Earth says:
"Wisdom is the mind
that keeps the mysteries of my body
in balance."**

## SETTING

The focus of this liturgy is on Sophia, a fascinating mystery at the heart of creation. *Sophia* is the Greek term for Wisdom and is used in the Septuagint, the Greek translation of the Hebrew Scriptures. The liturgy celebrates the presence and play of Sophia in the cosmos.

The space for this celebration can be designed in various ways to highlight the presence of Sophia as the artist-child, a designer-weaver, designing the intricate patterns of life on planet Earth. One option is to have a symbol of Earth at the center of the worship space surrounded by a mandala or spiral of natural things — seeds, flowers, crystals, sand — moving out from the center. Worshipers may extend the mandala with mysterious pieces of creation they have chosen.

Another option is to have a central web — perhaps a weaving — at the center of the worship space. From that center a complex of webs, like a rich tapestry of life, reaches out to form the complex webs of creation. Sophia is the source at the center and the thread that connects all the webs. The various webs could be the life patterns in leaves, ferns, crystals, genes, molecules, or ecosystems.

The intricate art of quilting has also been used to depict the delicate design and dancing combinations of Sophia at work weaving the fascinating fabric of creation.

91

Before the liturgy begins ask people to take the roles of Speakers 1, 2, A, B, C, D, E, and F. Divide the worship community into Groups 1 and 2.

## TEXTS AND REFLECTION

### Texts

The catalyst for this liturgy is Proverbs 8:21–31. A modern translation of this text by Norman Habel and Joh Wurst follows.[1]

### *Proverbs 8:21–31*[2]

*In the beginning YHWH gave birth to me —*
*the way that preceded YHWH's works.*
*From eternity I was installed,*
*before the beginnings of Earth.*
*When there were no deep waters I was born,*
*when there were no springs abounding with water.*
*Before the mountains had been sunk,*
*before the hills, I was born.*
*When YHWH had not yet made land and fields,*
*or the first clods of the world,*
*when YHWH was establishing the sky, I was there;*
*when YHWH was drawing a circle on the face of the deep,*
*when YHWH was condensing the clouds above,*
*and establishing the fountains of the deep waters,*
*when YHWH was assigning a limit to sea*
*so that waters might not transgress YHWH's command,*
*when YHWH inscribed the foundations of Earth,*
*I was beside YHWH, a designer-weaver,*[3]
*and I delighted YHWH every day,*
*celebrating before YHWH all the time,*
*celebrating YHWH's inhabited world,*
*and delighting human beings.*

---

1. On the use of "YHWH" see "The Text" on p. 59.

2. Texts complementing this key text from Proverbs 8 include Proverbs 3:13–20 and Job 28, especially verses 23–27, where God searches and finds Wisdom in creation and sets Wisdom in place for the wise to seek. Also significant is 1 Corinthians 1:18–30, where Christ is identified as the Wisdom of God. Proverbs 8 is frequently connected with John 1:1–14.

3. An alternative translation: "child-artisan"; this imagery may be more appropriate for some worship groups.

## Reflection, by Norman Habel[4]

### Preamble

The reflection that follows sets the scene for celebrating the Song of Sophia, a song of Earth. In this study I will lead listeners in an exploration of the biblical background and environmental context of Sophia's Song. I hope this reflection will help us sing this song of Earth with a fresh awareness of Sophia-Wisdom's presence in creation, especially on planet Earth. The text for this study is the translation of Proverbs 8:21–31 provided above.

### Past Readings

*Sophia* is the Greek form of the English noun "wisdom" — sometimes translated from the Hebrew feminine noun as Woman Wisdom — used in the book of Proverbs. Here I will use the Greek form, Sophia, to underline the subtle "feminine" double meaning that operates in both the Greek and Hebrew texts, where the noun, usually translated as the neutral noun "wisdom" in English, is understood as female. In this sense, the text is subtly and ambiguously referring both to a woman, named Sophia or Wisdom because she is wise, and an inanimate principle, wisdom.

The story of Sophia in Proverbs 8 is frequently read as a variation of the creation account in Genesis 1 and an elaboration of the statement that "YHWH by Wisdom founded Earth" (Proverbs 3:19). Sometimes a connection is made with the message of John's Gospel that all things are made by the Word (John 1). The focus in such readings is on God as the sole creator and Sophia (Wisdom) as an agent or vehicle God used to create this world. The work of God and Sophia tends to be viewed as an event in the distant past. When I looked more closely at the Hebrew text, however, I discovered that the focus is not so much on the acts of creation but on the presence of Sophia.

What does it mean when Sophia says she was/is "there" from the beginning of creation?

---

4. At its original celebration, this liturgy included the Reflection written by Dianne Bradley, a member of the Sophia community. The text of this alternative reflection is provided on p. 235. Groups wishing to use this liturgy should explore both alternatives and decide if either suits their purposes. Any group is free to use a Reflection written by a member of the group for this liturgy and for any other liturgy presented in this volume.

## *Reading the Text Again*

The text begins with the bold claim that Sophia is present from the very beginning. Although some people translate the verb in the opening line as "create," this is not the normal Hebrew word for create. This verb is more likely to mean "acquire," "birth/beget," or "bring into existence." It is significant that in the following verses, Sophia says she was "born" or "brought forth." The Hebrew verb used describes a mother writhing with birth pangs. So Sophia emerges, comes forth, is born, appears — and is "there" for God to discover. God is portrayed as a midwife.

Earth is that feature of creation that frames the story. It is mentioned at the beginning of the text block in verse 23 and at the end in verse 29. Within this Earth-frame there are deeps, springs, mountains, hills, land, air, and seas. This list covers the major structures of Earth — its geology and geography — from mountains to clods of soil. No living creatures are mentioned. But Sophia is "there."

What does it mean that Sophia is "there"? Is she a casual observer? an overseer? a helper? or something quite different?

One clue as to the nature and function of Sophia in this text may lie in the verbs associated with the way the world is structured. Mountains are "shaped"; heavens are "established in place"; the watery deep is contained within a circle; limits and boundaries are set for the oceans and seas; and the foundations of Earth are marked. This picture sounds like what we would call a blueprint or design for constructing Earth. Sophia is connected with that blueprint of creation in some way. But how?

Is Sophia herself the blueprint for Earth? Or something else? One text that helps us explore this question is Job 28, where the poet asks the famous question: Where can Sophia be found? Where is her place? After making it clear that humans cannot discover Wisdom of their own accord, the poet describes how God discovered Wisdom:

> God understands the way to Sophia,
> and God knows her place.
> For God looks to the ends of Earth,
> and sees everything under the heavens.
> When God gave the wind its weight
> and apportioned out the waters by measure;
> when God made a decree for the rain,
> and a way for the thunderbolt;

> then God saw Sophia and recognized Sophia,
> God discovered Sophia and searched Sophia.
>
> (Job 28:23–27)

A striking feature of this passage is the claim that God discovers Sophia in the process of ordering the structures or systems of creation — in this case the weather systems. God discerns Sophia in the laws, limits, patterns and ecosystems of nature. There is more to creation than a mechanical structure. Sophia is present like a secret code or hidden key to the mysteries of Earth.

If we return to the first verse of our text, Sophia describes herself as "the way" that precedes the works of creation. For the wise of the Old Testament world, everything has its "way" — whether it be the lightning or the eagle, the tree or the snowflake. And Sophia, Wisdom, is the "way" of the whole creation, the hidden code of the cosmos, the blueprint God used to construct the universe.

## The Song of Sophia

In Proverbs 8:30, however, Sophia is also described using a Hebrew word that can have two meanings: "artisan/designer" or "child." Perhaps a double entendre is intended. As a designer, a weaver, Sophia may be the creative force, the artistic impulse within creation, the one who wove all the patterns of life. As a child, Sophia may be the spirit of play in creation, the imagination that evoked the mysteries of Earth, the child that is yet unfolding.

Perhaps more important than how we translate this ambiguous Hebrew word is our understanding of how this figure is described: she delights daily and rejoices before God. Sophia not only makes things and determines their "way," she also sings, celebrates, rejoices, and delights. She is "there" in everything; she is the life of the creation party. Sophia is also the song in creation, the vibrant soul of Earth, the eternal impulse that moves God to love creation and creating. Here there is no hint of the cosmos as a giant mechanical clock that is winding down. Just the opposite! Earth is alive with celebration and is still being created.

# LITURGY: SONG OF SOPHIA

## Invocation

Sophia       Welcome, I open my heart to you.
Enter here, receive my love and compassion.

All       *Yes, Sophia, we enter;*
*we will partake of your generosity;*
*we will listen to your voice;*
*we will learn from your wisdom.*

Sophia       Welcome, I open my heart to you.
Enter here, receive my love and compassion.

All       *Yes, Sophia, we enter;*
*we will discern your workings in nature;*
*we will see your richness in Earth;*
*we will touch the rocks of creation.*

Sophia       Welcome, I open my heart to you.
Enter here, receive my love and compassion.

All       *Yes, Sophia, we enter;*
*we will dance in your house;*
*we will feast at your table;*
*we will joyfully sing your praise.*

Sophia       Welcome, I open my heart to you.
Enter here, receive my love and compassion.

**Song:** "Wisdom Song" (p. 149)
*(repeat as often as desired)*

      Wisdom weaves us
into Earth's growing:
singing, shining, resting, flowing.

Leader       Echoing song, breath of our breath, we seek you.
Give answer to our longing.

All       *Universal Wisdom, ultimate Mystery,*
*we follow your footprints.*

| | |
|---|---|
| Leader | Explosive freedom of creation, <br> burst our timid bonds, <br> and delight us with growth. |
| All | *Universal Wisdom, ultimate Mystery,* <br> *we follow your footprints.* |
| Leader | Pattern of Life, <br> steady flow of order and relationship, <br> we thirst for you — meet our need. |
| All | *Universal Wisdom, ultimate Mystery,* <br> *we follow your footprints.* |

*Everyone is invited to take symbols of Earth — leaves, nuts, pebbles,* *flowers, seed pods — from baskets being passed around the group. Keep* *them until these Earth symbols become part of the mandala formed later* *in the liturgy.*[5]

## Dramatized Reading of Psalm

| | |
|---|---|
| Speaker 1 | Wisdom writes in the ways of Earth; <br> I have been blind to them. <br> Wisdom dances in cyclical rounds; <br> I have tried to control her. <br> Wisdom weaves death into life; <br> I have tried to undo it. |
| All | *All the day long my disgrace is before me;* <br> *and shame covers my face (Psalm 44:15).* |
| Speaker 2 | I thought I should have what I wanted; <br> now the riches of nature are plundered. <br> The needs of my kind were my only concern; <br> now we are a plague on the planet. <br> I thought soil, air, and waters <br> were there for our use; <br> now they poison our children. |

---

5. Some groups may choose to include symbols that remind us of the destructive and polluting presence of humans on Earth. Bits of glass bottles, bottle tops, aluminum can ring pulls, bits of plastic and plastic lids can be used. For some worshipers, including these elements in the mandala tangibly reminds us that, because of God's grace in Jesus Christ, we bring our flawed selves to be healed through healing Earth.

I have acted unjustly to the first people,
who knew and respected your Earth.
Clever in defending our own,
we wounded the body of God,
which now bleeds our life.

All        *All the day long my disgrace is before me;*
           *my face is covered with shame.*
           *Wisdom, wash my dull eyes;*
           *refresh me with your astringent truths;*
           *delight me with your scented mysteries,*
           *your challenging music;*
           *and I will drink again your living waters,*
           *take root in the ferment of your breathing world.*

## Reconciliation

*Spoken by those present.*

Group 1    Sophia/Wisdom, we have often failed
           to remember your presence
           in the wellspring of creation.

All        *Give us new awareness of your presence.*

Group 2    As newcomers we have failed to hear
           the wisdom of the first people
           in their ancient ways of living with the land.

All        *Give us new awareness of your presence.*

Group 1    We have thought ourselves bound to rule other species,
           failing to recognize our interdependence.

All        *Give us new awareness of your presence.*

Group 2    We have sought to dominate your creation,
           instead of celebrating your generosity.

All        *Give us new awareness of your presence.*

Group 1    We have imagined ourselves in control,
           oblivious to the awful forces you inhabit:
           time, the seed, the cycle of seasons, catastrophe.

All        *Give us new awareness of your presence.*

| Group 2 | We have claimed to love nature, but have failed to pay attention to the natural world. |
| All | *Give us new awareness of your presence.* |
| Group 1 | We have watched whole species disappear, but have done little to preserve the variety in which you delight. |
| All | *Give us new awareness of your presence.* |
| Group 2 | We have destroyed the first people's ancient ways of living, and failed to respect their wisdom. |
| All | *Give us new awareness of your presence.* |
| Group 1 | We have degraded the land, and polluted air and water. We have brought about discord. |
| All | *Give us new awareness of your presence.* |
| Group 2 | Open our eyes to the delicacy of pattern, the riotous chaos, the rhythmic order, which you have woven from the beginning. |
| All | *Give us new awareness of your presence.* |

## Absolution

| Sophia | Be comforted. I am with you. I am Sophia, radiant and unfading. I am quick to make myself known to those who desire me; I generously reveal myself in life's path and meet you in every thought. |

## Readings

| Reading 1 | If Christians were to embrace the ecological model, they would not be doing something radical or discontinuous with their historical faith. On the contrary, they would simply be extending that faith to include nature. If we are to love God with our whole heart, mind, and soul, and our neighbor as ourselves, how, in continuity with that model, should we love nature? The answer is: with |

the loving eye that realizes that even a wood tick or a Douglas fir is a subject — that each has a world, goals, intentions (though not conscious), and modes of flourishing that make them good in themselves and not simply good for us. Surely, this is what the Genesis verse means: "God saw everything that God had made, and indeed, it was very good" (1:31a). This is an amazing statement. God does not say that creation is good for human beings or even, more surprising, good for me, God, but just good, in fact, very good. God is saying that nature is good in itself — not good for something or someone but just plain good.... Even God can recognize that something exists outside of the divine self — and that, as such, it is good![6]

**Reading 2**      Proverbs 8:21–31

**Reading 3**      Philippians 4:8–9

**Reading 4**      John 10:10

## Reflection

*Select from reflections provided or use your own reflection.*

## Quiet Meditation

## Earth Symbol, Earth Rite

*Participants move into the central space to create a spiral mandala of natural materials — leaves, nuts, seed pods, flowers, pebbles — chosen from the baskets passed around earlier. The Earth symbols are placed around the central Earth symbol.*

**Song:** "Cycle Song" (p. 148)
*(repeat as often as desired)*

> Loving, suffering, dying, rising:
> we live the cycle
> Wisdom shares.

---

6. Sallie McFague, *Super, Natural Christians* (Minneapolis: Fortress Press, 1997), 164–65.

## Earth Prayers

| | |
|---|---|
| All | *When we take time to listen, birdsong enraptures us.*<br>*Smell gum leaves, and drab suburbs disappear.*<br>*Lake Eyre in flood is a miracle of plenty.*<br>*Let us attend to what is given and rest from our weary round.* |
| | *Plunge in the blue sea, and our life is renewed.*<br>*The vast sky frees us, if we only look up.*<br>*To work in a garden is to be nurtured by nature.*<br>*Let us attend to what is given*<br>*and rest from our weary round.* |
| | *When we take time to drink, the water slakes our need.*<br>*When we eat thoughtfully, bread fills our emptiness.*<br>*When we reach out in love, community is formed.*<br>*Let us attend to what is given,*<br>*and rest from our weary round.* |
| Speaker A | Sophia celebrant sings us to worship<br>in a parrot's screech, the waterfall's splash;<br>inspiring visionary, source of raw energy. |
| All | *Let us dance to the beat of her drum.* |
| Speaker B | Sophia prophet calls out our names<br>in a baby's gurgle, the view from a mountain;<br>inviting delight and proclaiming pain. |
| All | *Let us hear her urgent call.* |
| Speaker C | Sophia teacher gives us her wisdom<br>in the pull of the moon, a volcano's fire;<br>midwifing awareness and voicing doom. |
| All | *Let us open ourselves.* |
| Speaker D | Sophia savior searches for us<br>in a friend's question, a failed harvest;<br>resonant with anger, coaxing with patience. |
| All | *Let us be found by Sophia.* |
| Speaker E | Sophia creator weaves the labyrinth of life<br>like a hungry spider, a patient mollusk;<br>pathway of intuition and mutuality. |

| | |
|---|---|
| All | *Let us follow in her way.* |
| Speaker F | Sophia sustainer prepares a banquet with us: <br> fresh fruits of Earth and sweet rock water; <br> generous with justice and hospitality. |
| All | *Let us feast with Earth community.* |

## Eucharist

*Use an alternative form if desired.*

| | |
|---|---|
| Leader | Jesus, Wisdom of God, Sophia, we gather as community. <br> Be with us as we make Eucharist for Earth, <br> with elements given by Earth. |
| All | *We remember that you called your followers, women and men, <br> to eat and drink with you at a supper prepared by women, <br> shared by all; that you loved celebration; that you invited the <br> marginalized to your feast; that you reached out to all people.* |
| Leader | Let us say together our Creed. |

### Creed

| | |
|---|---|
| All | *We believe that God is one <br> — though known by many names — <br> and loves us with a love beyond a mother's and a father's. <br> God is mystery, beyond the human mind, <br> yet nearer to us than breathing, or a lover's embrace. <br> God brought forth the cosmos and Earth, <br> all things, visible and invisible. <br> In the dance of divinity is Sophia, <br> essence of creativity, breath, expressiveness, <br> Word, Logos, Spirit, <br> moving with God from the beginning, moving with us now. <br> Sophia, Wisdom of God, is the secret of all creativity, <br> enabler of human creation. <br> Jesus expressed in human flesh Sophia's yearning to be known, <br> to embody the nature of love and reveal us to ourselves. <br> We believe that Sophia's spirit infuses all things on Earth, <br> and in all universes, from time before time.* |

*We thank you Sophia that we see in Jesus*
*your lively word made flesh,*
*affirming the goodness of creation in our bodies.*
*Serving love and justice he hung between Earth and sky;*
*his arms embraced the wide world.*
*Earth saw his pain and groaned deep, fractured.*
*And suffering with him,*
*accepted him into her dark embrace.*
*Like a seed, he waited in your expectant silence,*
*and in his springing forth to life,*
*you show us, Sophia,*
*the power of Wisdom to pass through death*
*in your endless desire for renewal.*

*In taking bread and wine at his last meal,*
*Jesus proclaimed the life of God in the fruits of Earth*
*and made each meal a celebration.*

All/Leader     *We remember that, on the night you were betrayed,*
*you took bread:*
*grain from Earth and worked by human hands.*
*After saying thanksgiving,*
*you shared the bread among your friends, saying:*

*"Take, eat: this is my body given for you.*
*Do this in remembrance of me."*

*When the meal was finished, you took a cup of wine,*
*fruit from Earth which brings joy and release.*
*And again saying thanks*
*you gave the cup to your friends, saying:*

*"Drink from this, all of you.*
*This is my blood of the new covenant,*
*shed for you and for many, that life may be abundant.*
*Do this, as often as you drink it, in remembrance of me."*

Leader     The meal is before us. Come let us share and remember.

*The worshipers gather into a circle. Those who are assisting the leader*
*break the bread into individual pieces and place them in two baskets,*
*which they hand to two people in the circle. The worshipers give bread*

*to each other, with an appropriate phrase such as "The bread of life." When everyone has taken a piece all say the following words as a sign to everyone to eat together:*

| | |
|---|---|
| All | Christ has died; Christ is risen; Christ is. |
| Leader | The meal is before us. Come let us share and remember. |

*Wine-filled cups are then passed to the people in the circle, who hand them to each other to drink and pass on (unless individual cups are used), again with a suitable phrase, such as "The wine of life." When everyone has finished drinking, all say the following words together:*

| | |
|---|---|
| All | We thank you, God, for your sustaining love. |

## Quiet Meditation

## Commitment

All     At the seed's core,
in ocean swell,
through jagged lightning
and the ant's track;
in giving and taking,
living and dying,
and in the meshing of all —
we believe we find you, Sophia.
As we strengthen our will to hope,
nurture our capacity to love,
search for our healing power,
find life at the heart of our communal world —
our energy comes from you, Sophia.
We will lean into your strength,
explore the wonders of your mystery,
and cherish the fragile, intricate, dark-bright world
where all manifests you, Sophia.

## Action

*The leader invites people to move into the center and choose an item from the mandala to take away with them while singing "Wisdom Song."*

**Song:** "Wisdom Song" (p. 149)
*(repeat as often as desired)*

> Wisdom weaves us
> into Earth's growing:
> singing, shining, resting, flowing.

## Blessing

*All*

> *Bless us with knowledge of loss,*
> *and the wonder of your plenty,*
> *as we share your work*
> *and know it for our own.*
> *Nothing is bitter in your company. (Wisdom 8:16)*
>
> *Bless us with belonging, Sophia,*
> *enfold our separateness*
> *into relationship*
> *with our kind — and all kinds —*
> *with darkness and day,*
> *and your serene twilights,*
> *for you pervade and permeate all things. (Wisdom 7:24)*

**Song:** "Center Song" (p. 149)
*(repeat as often as desired)*

> Turning years take us
> a spiraling way,
> and move us to know
> the center is love.

## Acknowledgments

The *Song of Sophia* liturgy was first celebrated on March 2, 2002. It was composed by a group of eight women associated with Sophia, an ecumenical Christian spirituality center, particularly for women, established by Dominican sisters in 1991 and run by them in collaboration with volunteers. The women involved with this liturgy are white, middle-class, middle-aged or older, living in Adelaide, South Australia. They wrote from their own point of view. It is understood that any other group using this liturgy is free to substitute their own particular local references or concerns where those given are inappropriate. This applies especially to the reflection: an alternative is provided on p. 235.

The space in which the liturgy is performed is, ideally, circular, with the Earth symbol in the center, surrounded by seating in two half circles, with aisles to allow procession to and from the central area.

The women involved in preparing the liturgical resources were Dianne Bradley, Robyn Cadwallader, Dawn Colsey, Fiona Johnston, Angela Moloney, Eda Payne, Glenyce Durdin, and Jennifer Wightman (facilitator).

All translations from the Bible were made by Dr. Norman Habel.

The absolution draws on Wisdom 6:12–16; Wisdom literature is paraphrased here and elsewhere in the text of the liturgy.

Reading 1 is used with permission of the author and publisher.

The copyright for the *Song of Sophia* liturgy is held by Sophia, Cumberland Park, South Australia. The copyright for the music is held by Glenyce Durdin.

# SIX

# SONG OF LIFE

### Earth says:
## "I want to be your partner, your beloved, not your mother."

## SETTING

The *Song of Life* liturgy focuses on Earth community and uses sections from the Song of Songs from the Hebrew Scriptures as the core text. This liturgy shifts the focus from God's human creation to all aspects of God's creation on Earth. The *Earth Bible* Project used the term "Earth community" to refer to this diverse and interconnected web of life on planet Earth. This label is inclusive of all creation on Earth, including those aspects of creation often overlooked in a human-centered perspective: landforms, seas, air, and the sand, pebbles, rocks, and minute particles on the surface of the planet as well as the molten center and the tectonic plates. Earth community includes every part of the planet and its enclosing sheath of atmosphere.

For some people in the Western tradition, "Earth community" is better known as "Gaia," the living cosmos that is our planet and all that dwells therein. *Gaia* is the Greek word for Earth.[1]

The worship space for this liturgy is arranged to reflect the life-giving presence of Earth. A large wooden or earthen bowl, placed in the center of the space on a raised pedestal, is filled with fruits, and seeds. The fruits used should, if possible, represent fruits over which humans have "watched," through storage and other forms of natural preservation, such as apples, peaches, pears, grapes, and dates. Seats for the human worshipers are

---

1. See David Suzuki and Amanda McConnell, *The Sacred Balance: Rediscovering Our Place in Nature* (Vancouver: Greystone Books, and London: Allen & Unwin, 1997); Kit Pedler, *The Quest for Gaia: A Book of Changes* (London: Souvenir Press, 1979); Anne Primavesi, *Sacred Gaia: Holistic Theology and Earth System Science* (London and New York: Routledge, 2000).

placed in a circle around the bowl of fruit and seeds. Small pots filled with soil, placed at the perimeter, form the next circle. If possible, the pots should be encircled by an outermost circle of vines, representing the vineyards of Earth. An explanation of the spatial arrangement and symbolism and of the optional *Tapete* ritual is provided on p. 206.

For the dramatic reading in the liturgy you will need five people to read the parts of voices 1–5, plus a man and a woman to read the part of God.

## TEXTS AND REFLECTION

### Texts

The catalyst for this liturgy is the Song of Songs 2:10–13; 5:6b–8. A translation of this text is included below.

### *Song of Songs 2:10–13; 5:6b–8*

> *[The beloved speaks:]*
> *My lover speaks and says to me,*
> *"Arise, my companion, my beautiful one, and come away!*
> *For, see, the winter is past,*
> *the rains are over and gone.*
> *The flowers appear on Earth,*
> *the time of pruning the vines has come,*
> *and the song of the turtledove is heard in our land.*
> *The fig tree puts forth its figs,*
> *and the vines in bloom give forth fragrance.*
> *Arise, my companion, my beautiful one,*
> *and come away!"* (Song of Songs 2:10–13)

> *I sought him but I did not find him;*
> *I called to him but he did not answer me.*
> *The watchmen found me*
> *as they were making their rounds of the city;*
> *they beat me, they wounded me,*
> *they tore off my mantle,*
> *those watchmen of the walls!*
> *I charge you, O Daughters of Jerusalem,*
> *if you find my lover — what shall you tell him?*
> *Tell him, I am sick with love!* (Song of Songs 5:6b–8)

## Reflection, by the Creation Theology Group

### Past Readings

In the past, church and synagogue have read the Song of Songs in two distinctive ways: as a celebration of the beauty and wonder of human love, and as an allegory for the loving relationship between God (the bridegroom) and Israel, understood as both the historical people and the actual land (the bride), or Christ (the bridegroom) and the church or individual soul (the bride). In general, the allegorical reading has triumphed within religious communities since it brings a missing "transcendent" meaning to the very Earth-woven Song of Songs text. But has something been missed by overlaying the erotic play of Earth community with externalized divine meanings?

The Song of Songs is marked by a variety of features that make it critical for our understanding of the interdependence, suffering, and joy of all creation, and the implications of this for our custodianship of Earth community. The lovers themselves compare each other to animals and plants, a clear sign of lives lived in close connection with other entities in Earth community. The humans in the Song work as keepers of the vineyard and shepherds of flocks and herds, as persons in city and country who delight in the life-giving rains and the bounty of the orchards and wild places. Only in this text of the Hebrew Scriptures and Christian Bible do woman and man call each other by the most intimate of terms: "my companion," "my sister," "my brother." Only in the Song is the voice of the female subject given full expression as one who desires, seeks, finds, enjoys. Only this text acknowledges that as woman belongs to man, so man belongs to woman. In this text, no species is the conqueror of all the others. In the Song, one gender does not overpower the other; both welcome insights into the paradise of Earth we might experience if we gave up our desire for domination and control.

The relegation of these themes to the drama of historical salvation does a disservice to this piece of scripture; in the Song the power of the divine is felt as an immanent force displayed everywhere in Earth. We need not wrestle with the gardens of the Song to force them onto a human time line in order to make them relevant to our lives as creatures of Earth and people of faith. Rather, we need to read the Song with the eyes of Earth, and with reference to the sins our own kind have perpetrated upon Gaia, the living cosmos that is our planet and all that dwells therein.

In the Song we see the lover peeking through the lattices and walls of culture. This earthen-shaped lover offers us a profound invitation, asking us to "Come away!" from interpretations of Scripture that have brought death-dealing doctrines of gendercide, genocide, and gaiacide. The Song beckons us to hear again the promise of reading Scripture from an Earth perspective and leave our anthropomorphic fantasies behind: "Arise, my companion, my beautiful one, and come!"

## An Environmental Disaster

Human beings desecrate creation in our own backyards, in our own "vineyards" and orchards, in our fields and paddocks, perhaps not on purpose, but through our carelessness, our heedlessness to the signals from creation. In the Western world, we continue to pour toxic chemicals into the ground and rivers; we continue to live in ways that are unsustainable given the resources available. Governments and politicians in Western countries allow the perpetuation of unjust economic systems that privilege the rich, "developed," consuming countries at the expense of the poor and the planet.

We in the West pursue relentlessly this injustice done to Gaia and to humans who live outside the developed, industrial West. The crisis of global warming may well bring floods that do quench the sparks of love (Song of Songs 8:7). The thinning of the ozone mantle that protects us from deadly radiation has profound repercussions for all that lives beneath our planet's sun. We hear the cries of Gaia, and yet we do not stop our destructive behavior. When we do pause to consider the desecration of the fruited land, we project that destruction outward and away from our own intentionality: it is the "little foxes" who spoil the vineyard we would control for our own consumption. We project our relentless desire for more — and its consequences — onto other members of Earth community. But what have the "little foxes" done, other than seek basic food for survival, as any non-human creature does? We human consumers want harvests with no tilling, fruit with no seeds, pure water without the work of digging wells. How long can the planet tolerate our greedy indifference?

## Local Context: Environmental Issues and Concerns

*The person sharing the reflection may invite members of the worshiping group to provide examples of local environmental crises and concerns or*

*other examples that will be familiar to the group. An example from the
local context of the writers is included below.*

For over a hundred years after its establishment, our little seminary in
Newton, Massachusetts, was set upon a forested hill. Our Native American students tell us that long ago, indigenous peoples sought out this
"high place" to perform rites that honored Earth and their connection to
Earth. But that time is long past.

Now, this hill, a home to many creatures, has been reclassified as an
"under-utilized asset" by those charged with its management, those who
claim "ownership" of the site. As a consequence of financial troubles that
were not of the land's making, our hill has been bartered away to developers who have taken away our trees; destroyed the habitats of wild turkeys,
badgers, rabbits, geese, skunks, and raccoons; and given us in return more
human urban development (housing for the wealthy and another educational institution). While these projects might be good and worthy ones —
though some question even this — the decisions surrounding them were
made without placing a high value on considerations relating to the needs
of a preexisting complex ecosystem. Such matters were considered, but
in an atmosphere of economic rationality, Earth community on our hill
lost out to the needs of the existing and future human communities. The
result: we created a habitat for humans — only. The "watchers" of our
walls have stripped away our topsoil, dragged our trees out by their living roots, and given us concrete and glass instead. Yet we continue to
look away from our own backyard, and blame the "little foxes" — inflation, poor investments, court costs — for the destruction of our former
vineyard.

What will save us all? Our commitment to love in all its beauty and
wonder — especially as made known in the figure of the suffering servant
of Isaiah and the Gospels, and the revelation of divine purpose in the
work of Jesus of Nazareth, the Christ the church confesses as co-creator
and life-giver. Our species needs to realize that we also have a role to play
as co-creators of this creation; we are agents of creation's regeneration.
We must make amends; change our behavior as well as our beliefs; re-
covenant to heal and not to harm, to care for rather than to tear down
the vineyard. We can no longer blame the "violence" of creation for our
own destructive actions. Like the lovers in the Song, we must fall in love
with creation again every day.

## An Earth-Based Reading: Key Themes

### Theme 1: A New Bride

In our reading of the Song of Songs, the "bride" is creation — Earth community, Gaia — our most intimate companion and the beloved of the bridegroom, God. The "watchmen" of the city, who appear in Song of Songs 3:2, 5:7, are humans, charged in Genesis 2 with the care and custodianship of creation in the form of a garden. The watchmen are the ones who keep vigil, who guard. They are the sentries or keepers of the gate; in cities in the ancient world justice was dispensed in the gates. They are the ones charged with tending to the needs and welfare of the beloved. The "drama" of the Song, then, becomes a story of the yearning of Gaia and God to once more become one in a seeking and finding of immanence and intrinsic worth. Humans and their salvific destiny in a history played out upon the land — but with their ultimate fate in some disconnected heavenly city — have been decentered in our reading of the Song. We are not at the center; we are not the focus of the land's interest. The survival of our species is not the only value or goal that an immanent God or Earth community recognizes as worthy of redemption and renewal.

As Gaia and God seek to come together, the human watchers play an ambivalent role. Gone is their commitment to their duty to guard the bride and ensure that she comes to no harm! Instead, these watchers end up beating and bruising the bride and stripping her of her protective mantle. This crime is made all the worse for the "insider" aspect of this violence. It is almost like incest or "date rape." Gaia knew and trusted us, as we were appointed by God to be her caretaker and protector. Human beings have failed to acknowledge the interdependence of creation and have failed to act responsibly to care for and protect creation. Far worse than our failure to guard Gaia is our role as the instrument of the violence done to the whole planet.

The setting of the lovers' joy is important: the Song is set in a garden of paradise, a paradise of interdependence between bride and groom. This means that what happened to the bride, Earth, happened in the "backyard," within the walls, inside, in the very place that is supposed to be "safe." Our interpretation of the Song and its relation to environmental crisis everywhere relies on this connection between Earth community and backyard, and our wayward desire to say that nothing is wrong, "not in my backyard." Environmental destruction is happening right in our own environs, literally under our very own noses, yet we persist in the belief that it is someone else's problem to solve, and that someone else is responsible.

Who will guard the bride Earth, if not us?

## Theme 2: A New, Real Vineyard

The vineyards, orchards, and gardens of the Song are not those of a human paradise, where food drops from the trees without the work of tilling and pruning. Rather, all these places constitute a paradise of sorts because in them humanity and creation work together to create and nurture the fruits of the land. It is the joint custodianship between human and land that creates the paradise. Bound together in a cycle of growth, decay, and renewal, these vineyards produce because we, land and people, work together to make it so.

In our reading, we reject the historicization of the land and its produce. The vineyards spoken of here do not, in the first instance, refer to the days of rest and renewal experienced by Israel on returning to their homeland after exile (according to the Jewish mystical traditions). Neither do the vineyards and orchards of the Song refer to the Christian church and its harvest of souls, which the apostolic watchmen of the church offer up to the bridegroom Christ for their own perfection of faith (according to Bernard of Clairvaux). The land and its creations do not need to be understood as referring to something more important, with that "more important" meaning always being assigned to human activities, histories, and understandings. These are real vineyards, real orchards, real gardens, and they need be nothing other than themselves to merit our attention and care. They are real; they can experience real threat to their existence. In the face of these threats to fruitfulness, human beings must become real caretakers and workers in the orchard, and not abusive watchmen pursuing their self-interest, concerned with preserving a human-centered status quo of meaning and worth.

# ECOLITURGY: SONG OF LIFE

**Song:** "For the Beauty of the Earth"[2]

## Invitation to Worship

*The invitation is called from the back or middle of the congregation.*

| | |
|---|---|
| Leader | "Arise, my companion, my beautiful one, and come away! |
| | For, see, the winter is past, |
| | the rains are over and gone. |
| | The flowers appear on Earth, |
| | the time of pruning the vines has come, |
| | and the song of the turtledove is heard in our land. |
| | The fig tree puts forth its figs, |
| | and the vines in bloom give forth fragrance. |
| | Arise, my companion, my beautiful one, |
| | and come away!" (Song of Songs 2:8–13) |
| All | *We come to you, beloved Earth, bride of God,* |
| | *Whole to our half, home to our kind,* |
| | *We seek you! We see you! We come!* |
| Leader | Feel the pulse of Earth, |
| | Gaia throbbing with life, |
| | and you will come to love |
| | creation as your kin. |
| | Touch a delicate leaf with your fingers |
| | and run them along the veins down the stem to Earth. |
| | Hold a quivering bird in you hand, |
| | and set it free to fly on the air that you breathe. |
| | Feel the feet of an ant |
| | running soft on the skin of the ground; |
| | touch, hold, feel the pulse |
| | and you will come to love Earth, |
| | your Beloved throbbing with life. |
| All | *Earth and all that dwells on Earth is our intimate companion!* |
| | *Earth and all that dwells on Earth is our beloved bride!* |
| | *Who is this that looks out like the sun,* |

---

2. "For the Beauty of the Earth": words by Folliott S. Pierpoint, adapted; music by Conrad Kocher, abridged. *Singing the Living Tradition* (Boston: Beacon Press, 1993), Hymn 21.

*radiant as the moon,*
*terrible as an army with banners?*
*It is beloved Earth,*
*our intimate companion:*
*wilderness and garden,*
*fountain and sea,*
*animal and plant.*
*We belong to our beloved Earth,*
*and our beloved Earth is part of us.*
*Come, bride Gaia, come!*

## Readings

Genesis 1:11–12, 22–25; Song of Songs 1:16–17; Genesis 2:4b–8; Song of Songs 2:14; 5:6; 2:15; Jeremiah 12:10–11; Isaiah 3:14

### A Drama of Readings

*The dramatic reading uses the texts listed above. Voice 5 should be read by a woman. We suggest that the voice of God be read in unison by female and male voices. If the male and female voices also represent two ethnic groups, that would add to the egalitarian "music" of God's word. Where the text depicts a prophet relating God's words to the people, we suggest leaving the oracle in the prophet's voice (read by a single male of female prophet's voice) since these texts purport to represent a particular person's perception of God's message to the people.*

| | |
|---|---|
| Voice 1 | Then God said, |
| Voice of God | Let Earth put forth vegetation: plants yielding seed, and fruit trees of every kind on Earth that bear fruit with the seed in it. |
| Voice 1 | And it was so. Earth brought forth vegetation: plants yielding seed of every kind, and trees of every kind bearing fruit with the seed in it. And God saw that it was good. |
| *All* | *All that God created was good!* |
| | *Ah, you are beautiful, my beloved, truly lovely!* |
| | *Our couch is green;* |
| | *the beams of our house are cedar,* |
| | *our rafters are pine.* |

| | |
|---|---|
| Voice 2 | And God said, |
| Voice of God | Let the waters bring forth swarms of living creatures, and let birds fly above Earth across the dome of sky. |
| Voice 2 | So God created the great sea monsters and every living creature that moves, of every kind, with which the waters swarm, and every winged bird of every kind. And God saw that it was good. God blessed them, saying, |
| Voice of God | Be fruitful and multiply and fill the waters in the seas, and let birds multiply on Earth. |
| Voice 3 | And God said, |
| Voice of God | Let Earth bring forth living creatures of every kind: cattle and creeping things and wild animals of Earth of every kind. |
| Voice 3 | And it was so. God made the wild animals of Earth of every kind, and the cattle of every kind, and everything that creeps upon the ground of every kind. And God saw that it was good. |
| All | *Behold, all that God created was very good indeed!* <br> *O Earth-dove, in the clefts of the rock,* <br> *in the covert of the cliff,* <br> *let us see your face!* <br> *Let us hear your voice!* <br> *For your voice is sweet,* <br> *and your face is lovely!* |
| Voice 4 | In the day that YHWH[3] God made Earth and sky, <br> when no plant of the field was yet in Earth <br> and no herb of the field had yet sprung up <br> for YHWH God had not caused it to rain upon Earth, <br> there was no one to till the ground; <br> but a stream would rise from Earth, <br> and water the whole face of the ground. |

---

3. On the use of "YHWH" see "The Text" on p. 59.

Then YHWH God formed a human creature
from the dust of the ground,
and breathed into its nostrils the breath of life;
and the human creature became a living being.
And YHWH God planted a garden in Eden, in the east;
and there YHWH God put the human creature whom
God had formed.

All        *There was no one to till Earth!*
*There were no watchers to guard the bride!*
*Dust of Earth's dust,*
*bone of Earth's bone,*
*flesh of Earth's flesh,*
*we were made to care for God's bride!*
*God made us from Earth to work for Earth!*
*God set us as guardians to watch over Earth-bride!*

Voice 5    The watchmen found me
as they were making their rounds of the city;
they beat me,
they wounded me,
they tore off my mantle,
those watchmen of the walls!

All        *Catch us the foxes, the little foxes, that ruin the vineyards*
*for our vineyards are in blossom.*

Voice 6    YHWH God says to me,
Many shepherds have destroyed my vineyard,
they have trampled down my portion,
they have made my pleasant portion
a desolate wilderness.
They have made it a desolation;
desolate, it mourns to me.
The whole land is made desolate,
but no one lays it to heart.
YHWH enters into judgment
with the leaders of the people:
It is you who have devoured the vineyard;
the spoil of the poor is in your houses.

## Confession

| | |
|---|---|
| Leader | Let us confess our sins against Earth, God's bride. |
| | We ripped into Earth's soft spots and beat God's bride. |
| All | *Earth trusted us.* |
| Leader | We have paved Earth's fertile valleys, and removed Earth's shawl. |
| All | *Earth trusted us.* |
| Leader | We have wounded Earth, drilling for black oil, because we were too greedy to conserve Earth's resources. |
| All | *Earth trusted us.* |
| Leader | We have bored into Earth's core for gems and coal. |
| All | *Earth trusted us.* |
| Leader | We have drugged Earth's water ways with pesticides and fertilizers. |
| All | *Earth trusted us.* |
| Leader | We have lodged large sores of toxic waste under Earth's skin. |
| All | *Earth trusted us.* |
| Leader | We have removed Earth's mantle of life-protecting ozone. |
| All | *Earth trusted us.* |
| Leader | We have sinned again and again. |
| All | *Earth trusted us.*<br>*Like a child, like our pregnant mother,*<br>*like an ancient crone,*<br>*Earth has not done otherwise . . . yet.*<br>*How long can Earth continue to trust us?*<br>*We repent, we repent!*<br>*We will no longer blame the foxes*<br>*for what our kind has done.* |
| Leader | From now on let us be true watchers |

who guard the bride of the Holy One.
Let us covenant this day to be true guardians to Earth.

*All*
　　*I am a flame of fire, blazing with passionate love;*
　　*I am a spark of light, illuminating the deepest truth;*
　　*I am a rough ocean, heaving with righteous anger;*
　　*I am a calm lake, comforting the troubled breast;*
　　*I am a wild storm, raging at human sins;*
　　*I am a gentle breeze, blowing hope in the saddened heart;*
　　*I am dry dust, choking worldly pride;*
　　*I am wet Earth, bearing rich fruits of grace.*[4]

## Song: " 'Tis a Gift to Be Simple"[5]

## Reflection

*The reflection can take various forms, including a "sermon," or dramatization based on the work of the Creation Theology Group writers presented in this chapter. The reflection could also be an art event such as a Tapete; see p. 206. If you decide to use a Tapete we suggest that a group be designated to work together to prepare the Tapete sawdust painting for its use in the liturgy. If the worshiping group is unfamiliar with the process, it may be appropriate for the worship leader or a designated person involved in its preparation to explain the process of making the sawdust painting, the reasons why the group chose each image, and the significance of dancing through the sawdust painting and dispersing the sawdust at the end of the liturgy. After the Earth Rite, the painting will be broken down and returned to its "cosmic" pre-creation state during the final dance that concludes the liturgy.*

## Earth Symbol/Earth Rite

### *The Vineyard Renewed*

*Place a large wooden bowl filled with bite-sized slices of organically grown local fruit in the midst of the congregation. Be sure that each slice has seeds and leave the seeds intact. Fill small pots with topsoil — enough for every person present, plus some extras for good measure — and place them at the outer perimeter of the worship space.*

---

4. The covenant text comes from *The Black Book of Cararthan*, a first-millennium text written in Welsh.

5. " 'Tis a Gift to Be Simple": words by Joseph Beckett; music American Shaker tune. *Singing the Living Tradition* (Boston: Beacon Press, 1993), Hymn 16.

*This bowl and its contents serve as a symbol of Earth: the fruit of the land, its vineyards, complete with their own means of regeneration — seeds of Earth's sustainable justice, too often tossed away as irrelevant by human consumers. If at all possible, the fruit should either be in season for the location of the liturgy or represent a local tradition of "keeping" (watch over) food — apples wintered over in cool storage, or grapes, cranberries, or figs that have been dried and stored.*

## Intention

Leader      Our Earth Communion Rite:

- connects worshipers with the fruits of the Earth that — unbidden — sustain us and our fellow land creatures;

Our Earth Communion Rite:

- recognizes that healthy, regional agricultural practices are important to the health of Earth, as well as to human health;

Our Earth Communion Rite:

- reminds us that human beings are agents of regeneration.

## Earth Rite

Leader      Earth has set her table and called us to come and eat!

All      *Therefore, let us keep the feast!*

Leader      Whoever eats of my fruit, says Earth,
that one is part of me.
Whoever shares my fruit, says Earth,
that one becomes my seed.

All      *Let us partake of Earth's vineyards!*
*Let us become Earth's seed!*

Leader      Come make it so in action.
Come eat, and plant your seed.

All      *Let it be!*

*The people come to the Earth symbol — the fruit bowl — and take a piece of fruit. When all are served, everyone goes to the outer perimeter and takes a pot of soil. When everyone present has a piece of fruit and a pot of soil, all eat their piece of fruit and spit the seeds into the soil in their pot. Each person holds the seeded pot during the Earth prayers and lifts the pot while speaking the affirmation of commitment.*

**Song:** "Song of Life" (p. 160)

### Earth Prayers

*The people offer prayers for and blessings of Earth, including any local environmental concerns that are troubling their hearts and their land. After each petition, everyone responds in unison.*

All          *Let it be!*

### Prayer of Commitment

All          *Great Spirit,*
*give us hearts to understand;*
*never to take from creation's beauty more than we give;*
*never to destroy wantonly for the furtherance of greed;*
*never to deny giving our hands*
*for the building of Earth's beauty;*
*never to take from her what we cannot use.*
*Give us hearts to understand*
*that to destroy Earth's music is to create confusion;*
*that to wreck Earth's appearance is to blind us to beauty;*
*that to callously pollute Earth's fragrance*
*is to make a house of stench;*
*that as we care for Earth, Earth will care for us.*
*Amen. Let it be!*

### Affirmation of Commitment

*While speaking the words of the affirmation, all lift their seeded pots in a "toast" to Earth.*

All          *God, Creator Spirit,*
*we, the children of Earth*
*recognize that we have exploited Earth,*

*but from now on*
**we promise Earth**
*that we will respect all its life-forms,*
*and celebrate them*
*as valued members of the Earth community;*
**we promise Earth**
*that we will care for Earth*
*as Earth has cared for us,*
*protect the Earth community from harm,*
*and preserve its resources so that future generations*
*will have healthy food, air, water, and soil*
*to live full lives;*
**we promise Earth**
*that we will struggle to overcome those forces*
*that keep members of the Earth community*
*poor, oppressed, and excluded;*
**we promise Earth**
*that we will use Earth's resources to sustain life*
*rather than exploit it.*

**Yes, we promise the Earth!**

Leader      Go in peace to love and serve Earth!

All      *Let it be!*

*All take their pots to the outer perimeter of the worship space and set them down outside the "dance space" of the sawdust painting.*

**Song:** "Joyful, Joyful, We Adore Thee!"[6]

## Dance for the Earth

*You may want to include a Tapete here. See p. 206.*

## Earth Action

*All take their seeded pots home to plant in their home gardens. The leader plants her or his pot within or near the worship space.*

---

6. "Joyful, Joyful, We Adore Thee": words by Henry van Dyke (1852–1933); music by Ludvig van Beethoven. *Singing the Living Tradition* (Boston: Beacon Press, 1993), Hymn 29.

**Recessional song:** "Let It Be!" (John Lennon and Paul McCartney)[7]

## Acknowledgments

The Creation Theology Group — Carole Fontaine, Mary F. Bettencourt, Colleen Brown, Alison Cornish, Heidi Haverkamp, Joy Honen, Vicki Keene, Deborah Lindsay, Tadd Morton, Katherine Orcutt, Matthew Paquette, Nita Penfold, Marilyn Richards, Jennifer Rossetti, Pamela Cady Spain, Brent Sterste, Bill Wildman, Jr., and Valerie Young — were members of the 2001 "Biblical Theology: Creation" class at Andover Newton Theological School, Newton, Massachusetts.

_____

7. "Let It Be!" by the Beatles, Capitol Records, May 1970 (song: asin b000002ub6).

# SEVEN

# SONG OF HEALING

### Earth says:
### "Place your healing hands on my wounds
### and share my pain."

## SETTING

This liturgy focuses on healing planet Earth. In *Song of Healing*, Earth is remembered as garden, the wild places of an unspoiled world, of a creation actively resisting the impact of human domination and greed. Earth is embodied, and a subject whose cries of agony are heard by prophets and peoples sensitive to the wounds and diseases of Earth. Through Christ, Earth is also the garden of God, the sacred-secret garden God created in Eden, in the beginning. Our task as Christians and members of Earth community is to be the agents of Christ in healing God's garden.

The setting for this rite of healing is a garden or forest. An earthenware or clay bowl, filled with soil/earth — the Earth bowl, symbolizing Earth — is placed in the center of the worship space. A garden of trees, plants, fountains, flowers, and similar living things surround the Earth bowl. At the center of the Earth bowl is the tree of life represented by an aromatic herbal plant such as rosemary.

At four points around the bowl are pedestals. During the liturgy, symbols of the four domains of the wild — Land, Waters, Rain Forests/Forests, and Mountains — will be placed on the pedestals. These domains can be symbolized by a mound of soil in a vessel (land), a water fountain (waters), a gum tree (rain forests), and an interesting rock (mountains).[1] A cushion for the symbol bearer to sit on may be placed in front or to the side of each pedestal; the cushions should be close enough to allow the symbol bearers to hold hands while seated.

---

1. Other symbols of these four domains of the wild may be more appropriate in a given location.

The readings begin with the wonderful world of the wild portrayed in Job, a vision of the unspoiled world at the beginning. In the second reading, the voice of Jeremiah confronts us with the voice of Earth in pain, experiencing sickness and injury in all four domains of Earth. As we listen to these words from the Scriptures, we as human beings can move from defending ourselves as arrogant rulers over Earth to an awareness of our need to listen to Earth and serve Earth rather than rule and dominate, to heal rather than hurt.

As listening servants, we are invited by Christ to come back into the garden, to the renewed Earth of Revelation 22:1–4, and become agents of Christ in restoring this Earth to the garden God intends it to be. The final rite of healing enables us to become agents of Christ in this process of healing Earth. We who lay hands on Earth in the ritual are called also to put our hands to work restoring Earth to health.

For the liturgy you will need five readers to read the words of Water, Land, Rain Forests, Mountains, and Jeremiah.

## TEXTS AND REFLECTION

### Texts

The background for this liturgy is found in a cluster of texts placed in juxtaposition. They take us on a journey from the unspoiled world of the wild at the beginning (Job 38–39), to the text that modern humans claim as their mandate for ruling Earth (Genesis 1:26–28), to an alternative text in Genesis 2:4b–15, where humans are created to "serve" and "care for" Earth. This text echoes the injunction of Jesus that we, like him, have come to serve rather than rule. The task of serving involves doing the work of Christ, who came to redeem and heal Earth as well as human beings. The translations included in this liturgy are by Norman Habel.

### Genesis 1:26–28

> Then God said, "Let us make human beings in our image and likeness to rule the fish of sea, the birds of sky, the cattle and all creeping things that creep on Earth." So God created human beings in God's image; in the image of God they were created; male and female they were created. God blessed them and said, "Be fruitful and increase, fill Earth and subdue it, rule over the fish of sea, the birds of sky, and every living thing that moves on Earth."

## Job 38:1–11; 39:5–12

Then YHWH answered Job from the whirlwind and said:
"Who is this who clouds my design in darkness,
presenting arguments without knowledge?
Gird your loins like a hero;
I will ask questions and you will inform me.

Where were you when I laid Earth's foundations?
Tell me if you have gained discernment.
Who fixed its dimensions? Surely you know.
Or who stretched out the measuring line over it?
On what were its pillars sunk?
Or who set its cornerstone
when the morning stars sang together
and the children of God shouted with joy?

Who hedged in sea with doors
when sea gushed forth from the womb,
when I wrapped sea in robes of cloud
and swaddled sea in dense cloud,
when I prescribed my limit for sea
by fixing bars and doors
and saying, 'Thus far you shall come and no farther!
Here your proud waves break!'

Who set the wild ass free
and loosed the bonds of the onager,
whom I assigned a home in the wild
and a dwelling in the salt flats?
An onager laughs at the furor of the city
and hears no shouts from the taskmaster.
An onager roams the hills for pasture
and searches for everything green.

Is the wild ox willing to serve you?
Will the wild ox spend the night beside your crib?
Can you hold the wild ox in the furrow with ropes?
Will the wild ox harrow the valleys behind you?

*Can you rely on great strength,*
*and leave your toil to a wild ox?*
*Can you trust a wild ox to harvest your grain*
*and gather it in from the threshing floor?"*

## Genesis 2:8–14

*Then YHWH God planted a garden in Eden, in the east; and there God put the human being God had formed. YHWH God made trees spring from the ground, all trees pleasant to behold and good for food; and in the middle of the garden God set the tree of life and the tree of the knowledge of good and evil.*

*A river was flowing from Eden to water the garden, and when it left the garden it branched into four streams.... Then YHWH God took and placed the human being in the garden of Eden to serve and care for it.*

## Reflection, by Norman Habel

### Past Readings

For Christians, Genesis 1:26–28 has been one of the most important texts in the Hebrew Scriptures. It has virtually stood alone as a mandate for the way human beings should relate to the environment and to Earth as a whole. This text has long been viewed as a divine right for humans to rule creation. This text has also been used in some Christian contexts as the basis for "harnessing nature" as if it were a wild beast, and exploiting creation as an endless source of supplies for human use. Many of the wounds suffered by Earth have been the result of human beings following the Genesis 1:26–28 mandate to dominate.

In more recent years, some biblical scholars have focused on the kingship imagery implied by the Hebrew word for "rule." Citing the model of kingship in Psalm 72, they have suggested that the implied emphasis is that humans should "rule justly" as God rules. Are these scholars correct? Does the text of Genesis 1:26–28 imply harsh domination? And if it does, should this text from the Bible be taken as the final word of God? Or should the message of Christ in the Christian gospel message override this ancient text?

### Reading the Texts Again

A close reading of the text suggests that the two key terms "rule" and "subdue" are harsh terms in other contexts and do not suggest just or caring control. In Psalm 72, the psalm used to argue for a just rule, the term "rule" in verse 8 is used in the context of foes bowing at the king's feet and licking the dust (Psalm 72:8–11). The term "subdue" has an even harsher connotation and refers to "crushing under foot" (Micah 7:19) and Joshua's "subduing the land of Canaan" by destroying the Canaanites (Joshua 18:1). In short, the key terms in Genesis 1:26–28, point to a tough text denoting the forceful domination expected of ancient rulers.

How should we respond to this text and the way it has been used to support environmental destruction? We could try to soften the meaning of the words "rule" and "subdue" to suggest that they really mean kind and gentle stewardship. But that approach still implies that humans are the "stewards," acting in the place of God as the ruler of Earth. And the dangers of a hierarchical approach to creation are still inherent in this model, no matter how benign the ruling that results.

A second approach is to explore the biblical tradition and consider whether other texts, largely ignored in the past, can provide alternative models and show us how to foster healthy relationships between human beings and creation in the twenty-first century. In this wider context, it is our challenge as Christians to determine whether Christ has spoken a word that supports or negates this text, as he has supported or negated other texts outside the Christian gospel traditions. For example, in the Sermon on the Mount (Matthew 5) Jesus overrides texts from Old Testament law. In place of "love your neighbor and hate your enemy," Jesus says, "Love your enemies" (Matthew 5:43–44).

### God's Challenge to Job

One of the most powerful speeches about creation — and presented as spoken by God to a human being — is the word from the whirlwind that God addresses to Job (Job 38–39). God challenges Job to be a "heroic human." God invites Job to demonstrate his power and knowledge and prove that he can comprehend and control creation. First, God takes Job on a journey through the domains of the physical world — through the land, the sea, the stars, the storm, the deep, and more. It is clear that Job is unable to grasp the laws of the cosmos, let alone control them. The world of the wild, the wilderness of the cosmos, are beyond the capacity of humans to understand, let alone dominate.

Then God takes Job into the wild of the animal kingdom, the domain of lions, ibexes, eagles, and wild asses. That domain too is beyond human domination. One text in this magnificent speech is especially significant. God challenges Job with two questions:

> Is the wild ox willing to serve you?
> Will the wild ox spend the night by your crib? (Job 39:9)

Here the verb "serve" is the opposite of "rule." If Job were capable of "ruling" in terms of Genesis 1:26–28, then presumably Job should be able to make the wild ox "serve" him and force a wild ox to lie down by his crib at night like a docile cat. Anyone who has had any experience with large wild hooved animals will understand how incongruous this image is — and the challenge it implies — for a human being!

Clearly Job does not rule creation or control the laws of the cosmos. And Job admits as much when he says, "Behold, I am small. How can I refute you?" (Job 40:4). In other words, this message of God from the whirlwind puts the mandate of Genesis 1:26–28 into perspective. In contemporary terms, it provides a reality check. Creation is not something to be dominated but to be revered as a complex incomprehensible mystery, a worldwide web of wonder and delight.

### The Other Mandate

The mandate to dominate in Genesis 1 is not only challenged by the voice of God to Job but is also countered by the injunction to serve in Genesis 2. God creates the first human from clay and thereby expresses a kinship between humans and Earth. The first human, *adam,* is made from the ground, *adamah* (Genesis 2:7). The trees, including the tree of life, rise from the same soil. A great spring also arises from the ground in Eden and branches in four directions across Earth. Humans are integral to the web of creation, one with Earth and one with life on Earth.

The relevant text is Genesis 2:15:

> Then God took and placed the human being
> in the garden in Eden to serve and care for it.

The two key words in this text are "serve" and "care for." They can also be translated as "till/tend" or "keep/protect." The first verb, while it may refer to tilling soil or tending plants, also means "serving," including serving in worship. When these concepts are placed side by side with the two key words in Genesis 1:26–28, we come to the striking realization that they are direct opposites:

$$rada = \text{rule} \quad \text{vs.} \quad abad = \text{serve/tend}$$
$$kabash = \text{subdue} \quad \text{vs.} \quad shamar = \text{keep/care for}$$

In the first two chapters of the Christian Bible, humans are given two mandates in relation to creation. Which of these two mandates should we follow: the mandate to dominate in Genesis 1 or the injunction to serve in Genesis 2? Which of these models is more likely to provide a healing ministry for creation?

## The Challenge of Christ

Which of these models is more consistent with the Christian gospel message, the message of God's free grace revealed in the cross? Consider the words of Jesus in Mark 10. The writer of the Gospel of Mark links the way we should live in the world with the way of the cross revealed in Jesus Christ. We should not be like rulers who lord it over their people or tyrants who dominate their lands. We should be "servants," like the "Son of Man who came not to be served but to serve and give up his life as a ransom for many" (Mark 10:45).

The implication of these words of Jesus is that we should be servant-disciples, like Christ: willing to work, even die, for the release of all who are oppressed and marginalized, whose freedom to live and flourish is not being respected or facilitated. And that includes creation as well as creatures, Earth as well as Earth community. And that includes every component of creation that has suffered human domination and greed.

After sharing this teaching, Jesus demonstrates his role as one who serves by healing a blind man and freeing him from darkness.

In *Song of Healing*, we confess that we have been part of the way of domination, and we ask Christ to make us servants of Earth. In that capacity we promise we are ready to be agents of Christ for healing Earth. And we commit ourselves to listen to Earth's voices and leave behind our human-centered ways of seeing and living on Earth.

## The Cry of the Forest

The need for Earth healing comes to us not only through the words of Jesus. It also comes directly to us from those parts of creation that have been wounded and torn. One such domain is the rain forests.

Rain forests in many lands have been destroyed without any reverence or concern for old-growth trees that not only convert carbon dioxide into oxygen for Earth community, but participate in mysteries of life and healing that we have not even begun to grasp. Some of the magnificent giants — mountain ash and myrtle trees in Tasmania — are hundreds of years old and up to twenty feet (six meters) in diameter.

For example, in 2002, in Tasmania near Mt. Arthur, the replacement of these old forests for cash crops involves burning old forest trees, aerial spraying the living forest growth with herbicides, laying poison to kill all browsing animals, and mass planting of seedlings alien to the area. Human greed has priority over the abundant and flourishing diversity of life in the Tasmanian rain forests. The complex natural biodiversity is replaced with a monoculture "cash-cow" crop. What survives of the forest is crying out in pain and grieving for the loss of life and kin.

### The Tree in the Garden

The crying forest with its healing trees calls us back to the original garden where the tree of life offers abundant life. The visionary text of Revelation 22:1–4 also summons us to the garden where Earth is renewed and the waters of life are surrounded by trees of life whose leaves offer healing for all peoples. In that garden, where Earth is being renewed, we return to the injunction of Jesus Christ to serve others, to use leaves from the tree of life for healing Earth and Earth community.

In this liturgy, *Song of Healing*, we are invited to move beyond the mandate to dominate. We are invited to confess what we have done to Earth through a blind following of this mandate, to return to the exhortation of Jesus to serve, and in doing so to become agents of Jesus in healing Earth.

# LITURGY: SONG OF HEALING

## Invocation

| | |
|---|---|
| Leader | God, Creator of every living form<br>in this garden planet called Earth, |
| All | *walk with us through this sacred garden*<br>*as you walked with our ancestors in the beginning.* |
| Leader | Christ, our wounded healer<br>suffering the pains of creation, |
| All | *lead us back to the tree of life,*<br>*to the source of healing for Earth.* |

Leader        Spirit of the wind and the whirlwind,
                breathing through every person and place,

All           *open our eyes to the mysteries of creation,*
                *as you did with Job long long ago.*

## Procession

Leader        As we sing the "Song of the Wild," we welcome domains of the wild to worship with us and share with us their story.

**Song:** "Song of the Wild" (p. 171)

*During the "Song of the Wild," four groups representing four domains of the wild — creation unspoiled by human hand — enter with symbols representing the domains of Earth: Land, Waters, Rain Forests, Mountains. They stand around the Earth bowl at the center of the worship space. At the end of the song, they place their symbols on pedestals surrounding the bowl and then sit on the cushions supplied, in a circle around the Earth bowl, holding hands and facing outward toward the worship group.*

## Readings

**Reading 1**      Job 38:1–11; 39:5–12
                   The Call of the Wild

*As these voices are heard, visual portraits of the four domains can be projected on walls or screens. As each domain speaks, the speaker stands, and the symbol is held toward the worshiping community. At the end of the speech, it is returned to the pedestal.*

Leader        Let us take a journey through the wild,
                to the world God showed to ancient Job —
                a world filled with wisdom and wonder,
                free from the dominating way of humans.
                Let us hear again the voices of the wild,
                speaking to us from their unspoiled worlds.

Waters        We are oceans surrounding your shores,
                the cool blue blood called sea,
                keeping the balance of moisture and life.
                We are the home to myriads of lives,

coral and dolphins and whales
that dance with God in the deep.
We are the voice of Earth in the wild.

Land

We are plains, deserts, scrub,
soil that sustains plant and seed,
the kitchen of Earth where food is supplied
for creatures that scuttle and screech.
We are the matter that matters,
the strong stuff called clay that binds us as one.
We are the voice of Earth in the wild.

Rain Forests

We are rain forests, filled with myrtle, eucalyptus, and ash,
ferns and the moss at your feet,
a deep green garden of life.
We are the source of living breath for Earth creatures:
oxygen that rises each dawn,
as birds bless our canopies with song.
We are the voice of Earth in the wild.

Mountains

We are mountains, boulders, rocks —
Earth bones that rise in the desert,
ridges that reach, reach up for the skies
and down to the lava below.
We carry the fossils of life gone before,
and delicate forms like lichen and moss.
We have innate wisdom — we know how to endure
the ice, the heat, and the quaking of Earth.
We are the voice of Earth in the wild.

All

*God, we hear your call from the wild,*
*and we rejoice in ancient mysteries*
*that form the intricate web of creation.*

**Song:** "Mother Earth, Our Mother Birthing" (p. 168)

**Reading 2**     Genesis 1:26–28

### Dialogue with Jeremiah

Jeremiah

I hear more than the call of the wild:
I hear the cries and groans of Earth,

cries of agony from land and forest and sea,
from bleeding birds and broken tree.

All  *And who are you to speak for Earth,*
*who are you to tell us what ails our mother?*

Jeremiah  I am the prophet who, long ago, spoke for God;
I am the prophet Jeremiah.
I am the one who hears the groans of Earth
and understands the pains in Earth's body.

All  *We are humans. We're the rulers of Earth.*
*We were told to subdue the Earth.*
*We listen to God, not to Earth.*

Jeremiah  It's time you learned to listen
to more than the sound of your own greed.
You are not rulers —
you are colonizing tyrants,
tearing the body of your mother apart.

All  *We are humans; we know all about pain.*
*Earth is not a human mother,*
*with a body that feels the pain we do.*

Jeremiah  You arrogant fools — How deaf you are!
Just because a body is not like yours
does not mean it cannot feel pain,
or suffer from disease or wounds.
I hear sea crying, and the waterways and rivers,
crying against the poisons and pollutants
that invade the veins of Earth.
The body of Earth has blood poisoning!
Can't you hear Earth's creatures crying?

All  *We are humans, not schools of fish.*
*Sea is for sailing, transport, swimming in —*
*And hiding human waste.*
*Why should we listen to the waves?*

Jeremiah  I hear the forests coughing, choking,
as vast tracts of trees are felled,

and the oxygen all animals need to live
is slowly depleted.
The lungs in the body of Earth are collapsing,
weakened by continuous burning and clearing.

All      *We are humans. We don't live in trees.*
*Trees are for timber, paper, and pulp.*
*Monkeys, birds, and bats live in trees, not us.*
*Why should we listen to bats or branches?*

Jeremiah      I hear sad laments from the land,
cleared of bush, scrub, and marshes,
where tiny brown frogs and bright blue birds
once sang in symphony.
The skin of Earth is diseased, a barren waste
with sterile salt rising to the surface.

All      *We are humans.*
*We think we are the superior species,*
*destined to control Earth.*
*The land is for crops, cows, and car parks.*
*How can we listen to toads or frogs?*

Jeremiah      I hear the groans of mountains in pain,
the aches of deserts and hills,
suffering from nuclear blasts
that release rays that can harm life for thousands of years.
Earth is suffering from deadly nuclear viruses
released deep in Earth's bones.

All      *We are humans.*
*We think that we can control Earth*
*with our human power and knowledge.*
*But we have lost the art of listening,*
*learning what Earth has suffered*
*because of our arrogant ways.*
*Creator God, teach us to listen to Earth.*

Leader      Jesus Christ has heard your confession,
your willingness to admit your arrogance as humans,
and your stubborn belief that you must dominate.
Now Christ invites you to hear his word,

first spoken in the sacred garden in Eden,
and during his human life in Palestine:
that you are called to serve, not to rule.
Yes, you are called to serve Earth as Christ served you.

**Reading 3**    Genesis 2:4b–10, 15
                  Mark 10:41–45

**Song:** "God's Sacred Secret Garden" (p. 174)

*The Message of the Garden*

*The symbol bearers each speak for the domains of Earth they represent: Land, Rain Forests, Waters, and Mountains. As before, they stand and hold their symbol toward the worship group as they speak. They replace the symbol on the pedestal when they have finished speaking.*

Land
              I am there with God in the garden;
              I am the soil, the *adamah* from which *adam*,
              the first human, and all flesh were made.
              I am still there, actively participating in
              the mysteries of life in plants and animals.
              I invite you back to the garden,
              the sacred secret garden of God.

Rain Forests:
      I am there with God in the garden,
      I am trees planted for food, for shelter, for beauty —
      and for making humans face their future.
      I am still there, actively participating in
      the mysteries of life for breath and growth.
      I invite you back to the garden,
      the sacred secret garden of God.

Waters
          I am there with God in the garden.
          I flow from the garden, from the tree of life,
          in all directions toward sea, the source of all waters.
          I am still there, actively participating —
          the spring of life and healing for all.
          I invite you back to the garden,
          the sacred secret garden of God.

Mountains
     I am there with God in the garden,
     I am the ancient mountain where Eden nestles,

the peak from which the rivers flow,
the rocks that hide the gems of Earth.
I am still there, actively participating —
a climate-modifier, and haven for many.
I invite you back to the garden,
the sacred secret garden of God.

Leader  I speak for Christ.
I too am there in the garden with God.
I am there from the beginning, and
I am living wisdom for all creation.
I am the tree of life to all who come to me
for forgiveness and life.
I am the water of life for all who come to me
for health and healing.
And I am the one who gave his life in serving,
to bring life, hope, and healing.
I am the way to the garden.
I invite you to come with me and serve,
to drink, to eat, to breathe life,
and to join me in healing Earth.

All  *We will come and serve with you.*
*We will eat and drink.*
*We will breathe life.*
*We will join with you in healing Earth.*

Leader  Then come. The garden is waiting.
Christ is present: the way is here.
Earth is waiting.

## Prayers for the Day

*Prayers relevant to the local group and context may be included here.*

## Blessing from the Garden

*The Eucharist from the* Song of Earth *liturgy (p. 54) or "Healing Eucharist" (p. 197) may be added here or used in place of "Blessing from the Garden."*

*In "Blessing from the Garden," people in the group move slowly through the garden along a designated path, meditatively pausing and praying as they choose, while appropriate music or forest sounds are played. The worship leader takes up a position next to the Earth bowl with the tree of life, holding a bowl of fruit or nuts, containing enough pieces for the members of the worshiping group. A bowl filled with small pieces of an aromatic herb such as rosemary is placed on a pedestal next to the leader. As each person passes the tree of life, the leader offers a piece of fruit, such as a grape, or a nut, with the words, "Take and eat. The gift of life from Christ, the tree of life." Before returning to their places the worshipers are directed past the bowl of rosemary on the pedestal and are invited to take a few leaves of rosemary and hold them as they return to their places.*

Leader          As you walk through the trees in your place —
be they ancient myrtle, giant ash,
eucalyptus scrub, or garden roses —
may they bless you with their breath,
cover you with their shade,
heal you with their balm,
touch you with their spirit,
and link your spirit with Jesus, the tree of life
who restores life to all creation.

*All*          *Shalom.*
*Shalom from Jesus, the tree of life for all creation.*

*Worshipers may wish to pass the peace with the words "Shalom" or "Shalom from Christ."*

**Reading 4**     Revelation 22:1–4

**Song:** "Song of Healing" (p. 166)

**Earth Healing Rite**

*If the Eucharist rather than the Blessing from the Garden has been celebrated, rosemary leaves may be distributed as worshipers leave the Eucharist distribution point, or they may be distributed during the preceding song. In this rite, the aroma of this herb on human hands symbolizes their function as healing hands.*

Leader          I invite you now to crush the leaves in your hands
to release the fragrance of life,
the aroma of healing;

|  |  |
|---|---|
|  | and as you do, |
|  | respond with the words: "the aroma of healing." |
| *All* | *The aroma of healing.* |
| Leader | As you inhale this aroma, |
|  | I invite you to remember the healing gifts of Earth: |
|  | penicillin and soothing balm, |
|  | clays, oils, and ointments, |
|  | and crushed leaves that release old remedies. |
|  | As you put your hands to your face and inhale, |
|  | respond with the words: "We remember, we remember." |
| *All* | *We remember, we remember.* |
| Leader | As you celebrate this aroma, |
|  | I invite you to remember the healing hands of |
|  | Jesus Christ, our wounded healer, |
|  | who suffers the pains of Earth — |
|  | the clay he smeared in healing on blind eyes. |
|  | I invite you to remember |
|  | the fragrant ointment poured on his head — |
|  | a loving preparation for his dying — |
|  | in the house of Simon the leper; |
|  | and respond with the words: |
|  | "We remember, we remember." |
| *All* | *We remember, we remember.* |
| Leader | I invite you now to become the hands of Jesus, |
|  | to let the healing power of Jesus Christ |
|  | flow through your hands. |
|  | If you are willing, respond with the words: |
|  | "These hands are the healing hands of Jesus." |
| *All* | *These hands are the healing hands of Jesus.* |
| Leader | Come to the living Earth before us, |
|  | still sharing the gifts of healing, |
|  | but wounded and abused by cruel hands; |
|  | torn and mutilated by greedy hands; |
|  | a Mother suffering at human hands — |
|  | the hands of her human children. |

As you come to the Earth bowl, say the words:
"We come to you, Earth, with healing in our hands."

All           *We come to you, Earth, with healing in our hands.*

*The members of the group each come to the Earth bowl, several at a time, and lay their hands on, in, and around the soil in the bowl. As they do so, they repeat the words: "We come to you, Earth, with healing in our hands." Before they leave, the leader, making the sign of the cross, says the following blessing aloud and dismisses each group.*

Leader      May the healing power of the risen Christ,
who is the tree of life in the midst of Earth,
flow through your hands
to heal the wounds in creation,
to ease the sufferings of Earth,
and to restore Shalom to this planet:
the rich aroma of life in its fullness.
Together we confirm this healing blessing
with the response: "Shalom, Earth, Shalom!"

All           *Shalom, Earth, Shalom!*

**Song:** "Rise, Creator Spirit, Rise" (p. 180)

# Part Two

# EARTH SONGS

## INTRODUCTION

The songs in this collection were all written after 1996. They reflect the new Earth-consciousness associated with the *Earth Bible* Project and with Earth-affirming communities. Each song was written in the context of a particular liturgy or worship situation and focuses on an Earth theme. These themes are central aspects of the liturgies included in the *Seven Songs of Creation*.

While these songs are especially appropriate when celebrating a "Season of Creation," they are also suitable for use throughout the liturgical year in worship contexts that reflect an awareness of the living world around us.

A major difference between most of these songs and traditional hymns that praise God for creation is that they involve all creation in the celebration — trees, animals, mountains, waters, and so on. The songs reflect an awareness of God's presence in Earth and Earth as a sanctuary, a living entity, a force at work in our lives. These songs invite us to listen to Earth, to learn from Earth, and to celebrate with Earth community. The Earth language of these songs is more than poetic expression; it is designed to evoke the presence of Earth and Earth community as an integral part of, another significant voice in, our worshiping community.

Norman Habel has written the lyrics to all but one of these songs. The songs are sometimes set to traditional melodies from known hymns and songs to facilitate their immediate use. Where new melodies have been written, worshipers have a choice of using the new melody or the traditional melody.

## CONTEXTUAL INFORMATION

### Song of Sanctuary (p. 146)

This song is a deliberate rewriting of the well-known hymn "Guide Me, O Thou Great Jehovah," a traditional hymn that devalues Earth and directs the eyes of the worshiper to heaven. Instead of viewing heaven as our true home, "Song of Sanctuary" affirms Earth as our true home — the sanctuary chosen for us to live in, and for God to fill with God's own glory.

### Song of Sky (p. 150)

In this song we are faced with the amazing reality of the vast and over-whelming cosmos, a sky beyond human imagination. Within that vast sky, one piece of stardust, Earth, is chosen by God to be the birthplace of life, the location for the presence of God, and the splendor of the cosmos. That humans should raid such a beautiful sacred place is even more amazing.

### Song of Earth (p. 152)

This song is a celebration of Earth, that mysterious domain first revealed by God in the beginning, when God summoned Earth to appear from beneath the waters (Genesis 1:9). In this song the mystery, wonder, and honor invested in Earth are proclaimed loud and strong. This song has all the joy of a resurrection cry and can be sung to the melody of "Jesus Christ is Risen Today."

### Song of Waters (p. 154)

"Song of Waters" is a fresh rendering of Psalm 104, focusing on the way God celebrates water in a rich range of forms. The invitation in this song is not only to sing about these life-giving waters, but to experience the waters and the presence of God in, with, and under these waters. I am open to someone writing another melody — in fact, I would be delighted! The traditional melody used here is "Praise My Soul the King of Heaven," a song tune that complements the invitation to celebrate the God of Waters.

### Song of Sophia (p. 156)

This song was written by Norman Habel for the Song of Sophia liturgy prepared and celebrated by the Sophia Community in Adelaide, Australia. The song is an expression of the profound mystery of Sophia (Wisdom) present with God at creation, now embedded in creation and celebrating life with each of us as we dance the songs of creation. The striking melody is the inspired work of Alan Cadwallader, a musician and New Testament scholar.

## Song of Life (p. 160)

"Song of Life" was written by Carole Fontaine, an Old Testament and feminist scholar. She wrote this song in connection with the Creation Theology Group in Newton, Massachusetts. The song captures, in a unique way, the spirit and joy of the physical dimension of life. The song is based on themes of the Song of Songs, where Earth is understood as the beloved who is calling us to join in a celebration of life.

## Song of Healing (p. 166)

This Earth song was created by Norman Habel in Geneva, where a team of Lutherans from around the world were meeting to write materials for the 2003 Lutheran World Federation assembly in Winnipeg, Canada. Healing was the theme for the assembly; the song captures key themes and images of healing expressed by writers on the team.

## Mother Earth, Our Mother Birthing (p. 168)

The occasion for this song was the fortieth anniversary of the ordination of Rev. John Sabel, a poet and a disciple of Saint Francis of Assisi. The poem honors Saint Francis by acclaiming Earth, Air, Water, and Fire as our kin, components we have in common with planet Earth and with Jesus of Nazareth. In addition, or as an alternative, to the rich melody written by Doug Petherick, singers may wish to use the traditional tune "Praise My Soul the King of Heaven," also included.

## Song of the Wild (p. 171)

This song is an exploration of the domains of Earth portrayed in the great speech of God from the whirlwind in Job 38–39. These domains are the world of the wild, the mysterious world that humans can only begin to understand but never master. The melody was written by Norman Habel's teenage daughter, Anjali.

### God's Sacred Secret Garden (p. 174)

This song celebrates Earth as a garden, as a sacred site, as a sanctuary, and as a place of love and promise. There are several connotations to the expression "sacred secret" — a sanctuary that is filled with mysteries from the hand of the Creator and a deep hidden truth that we are privileged to know. Among Indigenous peoples, the "sacred secret" story or symbol is revealed only to the initiated. The music is by Australian songwriter Leigh Newton.

### Hear This Earth Mourning (p. 178)

In this song we are summoned to hear the cries of Earth, every cry and sigh from the voice of the forest to the blood of innocent children crying from the ground. There is a subtle interplay with the words and traditional melody of "Morning Has Broken."

### Rise, Creator Spirit, Rise! (p. 180)

The words of this song were written in a workshop with the Rainbow Spirit Elders of North Queensland in Australia, who have redeemed their beliefs in the Creator Spirit — also known as the Rainbow Spirit — as consistent with their Christian faith. These words reflect their experience of God and all life emerging from Earth below rather than descending from heaven above. The Dreaming is the life force that emerged at creation, comes alive in sacred ceremony, and is shared by humans and other living creatures. The popular melody was chosen by the elders as one they love and a tune that is familiar to many Indigenous Christians.

### One Earth (p. 182)

This theme song was written by Norman Habel for the South Pacific Earth Charter Conference in Brisbane, November 2001. The song celebrates Earth as the one home we all share — all biotic and non-biotic life — and, through the Earth Charter, a home we are committed to sustain and respect. Nathaniel Ford, who wrote the melody, conducted a Soka Gokkai choir at the conference to launch the song.

### Celebrate the Land (p. 188)

This song, and the delightful melody written by Australian singer and songwriter Leigh Newton, is designed to help us reconnect with the land and our joyous kinship with all creation throughout the land. In the spirit of Psalm 104 and my Indigenous Australian brothers and sisters, I celebrate the land and the serendipity and beauty of life from the land.

## Liturgical Refrains

Music is also provided for several liturgical refrains used at various points in the liturgies and celebrated successfully in various countries. Sometimes it is useful to have a choir or music team lead these refrains.

Doug Petherick wrote the music for the refrains "Wonderful" (p. 187), "I Groaned" (p. 177), and "Sanctus" (p. 165). They were first sung as part of the *Song of Earth* liturgy in Adelaide, Australia.

The music for the three refrains from the *Song of Sophia* liturgy — "Cycle Song" (p. 148), "Center Song" (p. 149), and "Wisdom Song" (p. 149) — was written by Glenyce Durdin and first celebrated in the Sophia Community of Australia.

# SONG OF SANCTUARY

Words: © 2000 Norman Habel

Music: J. Hughes (1873 - 1932)

You who watch the high-est heav-ens Wond'-ring where God's man-sions are;

You who hope to spot an an-gel Spin-ning like a fall-ing star;

Earth is call-ing, Earth is call-ing, Come back home and rest in

me. Come back home and rest in me.

# SONG OF SANCTUARY

1. You who watch the highest heavens
   Wond'ring where God's mansions are;
   You who hope to spot an angel
   Spinning like a falling star;
   Earth is calling,
   Earth is calling,
   Come back home and rest in me.
   Come back home and rest in me.

2. You who build exotic buildings
   Taller than the forest tree,
   Don't you know that all foundations
   Deep, deep down reside in me?
   Earth is calling,
   Earth is calling,
   Come back home and live in me.
   Come back home and live in me.

3. You who travel Earth as pilgrims,
   Dreaming where you'd rather be;
   God's own glory fills my body,
   I am God's own sanctuary.
   Earth is calling,
   Earth is calling,
   Come back home to God in me.
   Come back home to God in me.

4. You who hope for joys in heaven,
   Do you know the joys of Earth?
   Ancient forests filled with singing,
   seas that shout when whales give birth?
   Earth is calling,
   Earth is calling,
   Come back home and sing with me.
   Come back home and sing with me.

5. You who long for bread like manna
   Falling from the hand of God,
   Know that Earth provides your water,
   Precious breath and daily food.
   Earth is calling,
   Earth is calling,
   Come back home and dine with me.
   Come back home and dine with me.

Words: © 2000 Norman Habel

# CYCLE SONG

Seven Songs of Creation: Cycle Song

# WISDOM SONG

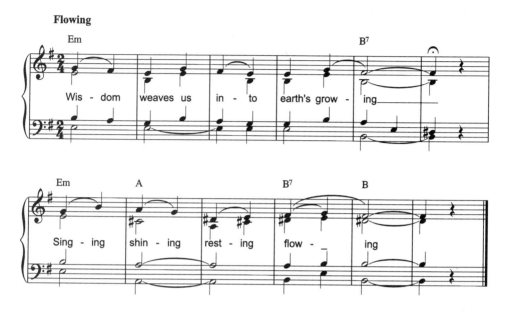

Wis - dom weaves us in - to earth's grow - ing

Sing - ing shin - ing rest - ing flow - ing

# CENTER SONG

Turn - ing years take us a spi - rall - ing way and move us to know the cen - ter is love

Turn - ing years take us a spi - rall - ing way and move us to know the cen - ter is love

# SONG OF SKY

Words: © 1999 Norman Habel

Music: Cyril Vincent Taylor

Lord of suns and stars ex - plod - ing Gal - ax - ies and
swirl - ing skies, Where you chose to show your glor - y Took the
hea - vens by sur - prise. Lord of so - lar winds and wis - dom,
Su - per stars that blow our mind, Choos - ing such a
frag - ile pla - net Hard - ly seems a grand de - sign.

# SONG OF SKY

1. Lord of suns and stars exploding
   Galaxies and swirling skies,
   Where you chose to show your glory
   Took the heavens by surprise.
   Lord of solar winds and wisdom,
   Super stars that blow our mind,
   Choosing such a fragile planet
   Hardly seems a grand design.

2. On this piece of stardust swirling,
   On this spinning spot in space,
   Life itself was born like music,
   When you showed your hidden face.
   What an honor to be chosen,
   Silent planet blue and green,
   Filled with glory, grace, and gardens
   Where the breath of God is seen.

3. Lord, your glory fills our planet,
   Breaking through with every dawn,
   Bursting from cocoons in hiding
   Where new butterflies are born.
   Searing fire in deep volcanoes,
   Rainbow arcs across the land
   Sign to us that God is present
   In the finest grain of sand.

4. What is even more amazing
   We have poisoned Earth like fools.
   Help us change our way of living,
   Love the Earth and love her rules.
   Help us stem the tide of traders
   Leaving Earth an empty store;
   Join us now Creator Spirit,
   Come renew your Earth once more.

Words: © 1999 Norman Habel

# SONG OF EARTH

*Words: © 1999 Norman Habel*

*Music: Anon. (Lyrica Davidica 1708)*

Hail the earth that first appeared, Alleluia

When a word from God was heard, Alleluia

Let the Earth arise and be, Alleluia

Filled with loving mystery, Alleluia.

# SONG OF EARTH

1. Hail the Earth that first appeared, Alleluia
   When a word from God was heard, Alleluia
   Let the Earth arise and be, Alleluia
   Filled with loving mystery, Alleluia.

2. Hail the rainbow flying high, Alleluia
   Spun by God across the sky, Alleluia
   Giving Earth a solemn word, Alleluia
   Never to unleash a flood, Alleluia.

3. Hail the planet blue and green, Alleluia
   Where the face of God is seen, Alleluia
   Glory filling all the Earth, Alleluia
   Celebrating every birth, Alleluia.

4. Hail our body made in clay, Alleluia
   Given breath to praise and pray, Alleluia
   Clay God honored by his birth, Alleluia
   As a human life on Earth, Alleluia.

5. Hail the groans of Earth in pain, Alleluia
   From the weight of human sin, Alleluia
   Longing for the Christ who died, Alleluia
   All creation to revive, Alleluia.

Words: © 1999 Norman Habel

# SONG OF WATERS

*Words: © 2000 Norman Habel*

*Music: J. Goss (1800 - 1880)*

Watch once more the wind-swept storm clouds; Sud- den - ly the sky has wings! God has come to rain a - mong us, Giv - ing hope to all dry things. Sing a song of splash- ing wa - ters, Puls- ing through the veins of Earth.

# SONG OF WATERS

1. Watch once more the windswept storm clouds;
   Suddenly the sky has wings!
   God has come to rain among us,
   Giving hope to all dry things.
   Sing a song of splashing waters,
   Pulsing through the veins of Earth.

2. Taste the moisture of the morning,
   Smoother than the best red wine;
   Toast the lifeblood of the planet:
   Here's to God's wild wet design!
   Sing a song of flowing waters,
   Pulsing through the veins of Earth.

3. View anew the dark blue ocean,
   Whales cavorting, spraying foam;
   God at play with deep sea monsters,
   Feeling very much at home.
   Sing a song of laughing waters,
   Pulsing through the veins of Earth.

4. Feel the breath of God move softly,
   Gentle mists that brush the skin;
   Earth is breathing God's own spirit,
   Life renewed from deep within.
   Sing a song of living waters,
   Pulsing through the veins of Earth.

Words: © 2000 Norman Habel

# SONG OF SOPHIA

Words: © 2001 Norman Habel

Music: © 2001 A. Cadwallader

C     Gm⁷     B♭maj⁷     Cadd⁹     C

Gm⁷     B♭maj⁷     Cadd⁹

Be - fore

C     Cm     Gm⁷   B♭maj⁷   Cadd⁹

star - dust was spun in - to plan - ets and suns   I was there; and be-

C     Cm     B♭   F   C

fore earth was born in the grey pri - mal dawn   I was there;___

2

# SONG OF SOPHIA

1. Before stardust was spun
   into planets and suns,
   I was there.
   And before Earth was born
   in the grey primal dawn,
   I was there.
   I am Sophia!

2. I'm that wisdom God saw
   in each natural law,
   I was there.
   I'm the myst'ry God found
   in each light wave and sound,
   I was there.
   I am Sophia!

3. When the world was created,
   we joined hands and we celebrated,
   I was there.
   Like a child when delighted,
   I got God quite excited,
   I was there.
   I am Sophia!

4. When the sages divine
   read the landscape of time,
   I was there.
   Saw the stars that were made
   when God's female form played,
   I was there.
   I am Sophia!

5. In each hidden design
   of creation you find,
   I am there!
   I'm the song, I'm the soul
   of all life that evolves.
   I am there!
   I am Sophia!
   I am! I am! I am Sophia!

Words: © 2002 Norman Habel

# SONG OF LIFE

*Words: © Carole Fontaine*                    *Music: © Shane Spangler*

Seven Songs of Creation: Song of Life

**Slower - Pensive**

For win - ter is past and we med - i - tate on

**Again Faster**

cy - cles of turn - ing from bar - ren to birth, of plant - ing and har - vest, of

griev - ing and mirth. O Beau - ti - ful One, will you come?

# SONG OF LIFE

Behold, my beloved, the sweet spring has come;
the orchards are greening with promise of food
that Earth will soon feed to all her wild brood.
Be like a gazelle on the spiced hillsides,
Leap over the mountains and peer through the grate,
    For winter is past and we meditate
    on cycles of turning from barren to birth,
    of planting and harvest, of grieving and mirth.
    O beautiful one, will you come?

The world bright with blessings can never be cursed
but ravenous creatures can work cruel hurts.
For we are the foxes that spoil all the vines,
until we repent, called by the Divine:
Creator, Redeemer, Sustainer of Life,
cleanse human hearts from our greed and our strife!
    For winter is past and we meditate
    on cycles of turning from barren to birth,
    of planting and harvest, of grieving and mirth.
    O beautiful one, will you come?

The green Earth cries out, Beloved Ones, come!
New fruits and dried, my children, I give you with arms opened wide.
When will you hear me?
When will you return to knowledge that my life and your life are one?
I am your gazelle; I am your Sacred Tree.
I am Love manifesting perpetually
    For winter is past and we meditate
    on cycles of turning from barren to birth,
    of planting and harvest, of grieving and mirth.
    O beautiful one, will you come?

Words: © Carole Fontaine

# SANCTUS

Words: © Norman Habel

Music: © 2002 Douglas Petherick

Boldly, Moderate Tempo

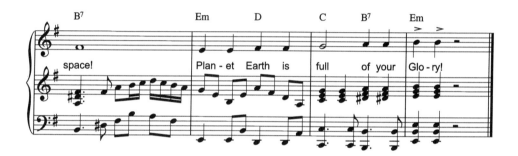

# SONG OF HEALING

Words: © 2001 Norman Habel

Music: Trad.

Seven Songs of Creation: Song of Healing

2

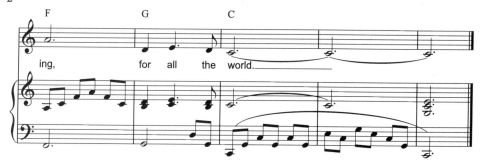

ing,       for    all    the    world._____

1. Healing is flowing, deep in the waters,
   Flowing from Eden, flowing from old.
   All through creation, God sends forth waters,
   Oceans of healing, for all the world.

2. Healing is rising, fresh with the morning,
   Healing is rising, bursting with grace.
   Christ, our rich healing, deep in creation,
   Heal Earth's deep wounds and rise in this place.

3. Healing is offered, leaves from the life tree,
   Healing is offered nations at war.
   Come, wounded Healer, torn by the violence,
   Rise from the grave, bring peace to our shore.

4. Healing is given, flows from forgiveness,
   Healing is given, flows from our faith.
   Christ, give us heart to love your deep healing,
   Living forgiveness, even in death.

5. Healing is hidden, crucified, hidden,
   Deep in the suff'ring Son on the tree,
   Christ, where you know abuse of our children,
   Come heal our homes where no one is free.

6. Healing is rising, free in Christ's body,
   Healing is flowing, free with Christ's blood.
   May this deep healing pulse through our bodies,
   Heal the world's wounds still bleeding and red.

# MOTHER EARTH, OUR MOTHER BIRTHING

Words: © 1999 Norman Habel          Music: © 2001 Douglas Petherick

Moth - er Earth our Moth - er birth - ing Ev' - ry
crea - ture from the ground. Je- sus too was flesh and
breath - ing, Kin to all that's green and brown. Cel - e-
brate with all cre - a - tion: God has

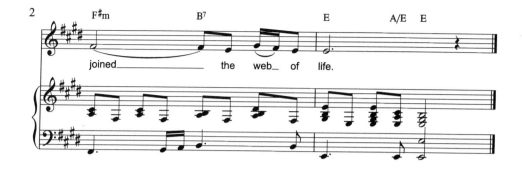

2

joined_____ the web_ of life.

1. Mother Earth, our Mother birthing
   Ev'ry creature from the ground.
   Jesus too was flesh and breathing,
   Kin to all that's green and brown.
   Celebrate with all creation:
   God has joined the web of life.

2. Sister Air, our Sister lifting
   Ev'ry creature born with wings;
   Jesus shared the breath of forests,
   Breath that makes our spirits sing.
   Celebrate with all creation:
   God has joined the web of life.

3. Brother Water, Brother pulsing
   Deep through ev'ry vein and sea,
   Jesus drank the very raindrops
   For our wine and in our tea.
   Celebrate with all creation:
   God has joined the web of life.

4. Father Fire, our Father burning
   With the sacred urge to live.
   Jesus' death completes the cycle,
   Bringing life beyond the grave.
   Celebrate with all creation:
   God has joined the web of life.

# MOTHER EARTH, OUR MOTHER BIRTHING

Words: © 1999 Norman Habel

Music: J. Goss (1800-1880)

Moth - er Earth, our Moth - er birth - ing Ev' - ry crea - ture

from the ground. Je - sus too was flesh and breath - ing, Kin to

all that's green and brown. Cel - e - brate with all cre -

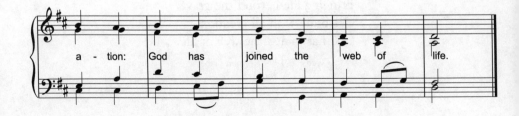

a - tion: God has joined the web of life.

# SONG OF THE WILD

Words: © 2000 Norman Habel

Music: © 2000 Anjali Habel-Orrell

# SONG OF THE WILD

1. Will you come back with Me to the birth of the Earth,
   Before all its life-forms evolved?
   Will you sing with the heavens amazed at the sight:
   A planet with secrets to unfold?
   > Will you praise,
   > Be amazed
   > With eyes as wide as a child's?
   > Will you praise?
   > Be amazed
   > And sing
   > The song of the wild?

2. Will you walk home with Me on my way through the wild?
   And watch baby birds break from their shells?
   Do you know how I serve as a midwife to all,
   The lion, the lizard, and gazelle?
   > Will you praise,
   > Be amazed
   > With eyes as wide as a child's?
   > Will you praise?
   > Be amazed
   > And sing
   > The song of the wild?

3. Will you gather with Me as the wading birds dance?
   Preparing to migrate north once more?
   Can you fathom the code I have fixed in their souls
   To navigate oceans when they roar?
   > Will you praise,
   > Be amazed
   > With eyes as wide as a child's?
   > Will you praise?
   > Be amazed
   > And sing
   > The song of the wild?

4. Will you sleep with your God in the desert one night?
   And wake with the creatures of the sand?
   Can you fathom the wisdom instilled in their mind
   To live without water, sun, or man?
   > Will you praise,
   > Be amazed
   > With eyes as wide as a child's?
   > Will you praise?
   > Be amazed
   > And sing
   > The song of the wild?

5. If you don't feel at home with the rain forest snakes;
   If you're troubled when the creatures change their skin,
   Then surrender the claim that you rule this Earth;
   And discover creation as your kin.
   > Will you praise,
   > Be amazed
   > With eyes as wide as a child's?
   > Will you praise?
   > Be amazed
   > And sing
   > The song of the wild?

# GOD'S SACRED SECRET GARDEN

Words: © 2002 Norman Habel

Music: © 2002 Leigh Newton

2

God's sac - red sec - ret gar____ den.

# GOD'S SACRED SECRET GARDEN

1. A million spinning galaxies
   A trillion orbs in flight —
   Yet God chose one to be a home,
   A sacred secret site.
   A million brilliant shafts of light
   Projecting into space —
   Yet God's own glory fills the Earth,
   A mask to veil God's face.

   This Earth!
   This Earth!
   God's sacred secret garden.

2. A million mighty forms are found
   Pulsating high above,
   Yet God let human form reveal
   God's sacred secret — love!
   A million ugly human acts
   May lay God's garden bare,
   Yet rainbows promise all of us
   The gardener still cares,

   For Earth!
   For Earth!
   God's sacred secret garden.

3. God chose a piece of common clay
   To share the pain of birth,
   To suffer with this broken land
   And heal the wounds of Earth.
   Now healing from the garden flows
   From Christ, the living tree,
   To lift the pulse of all that lives,
   And give them power to be

   This Earth!
   This Earth!
   God's sacred secret garden.

   Words: © 2002 Norman Habel

# I GROANED

Words: © Norman Habel

Music: © 2002 Douglas Petherick

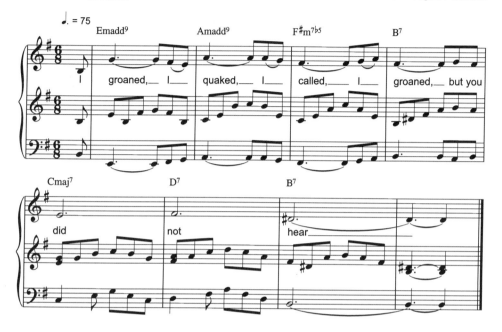

# HEAR THIS EARTH MOURNING

Words: © 2000 Norman Habel

Music: Trad.

2

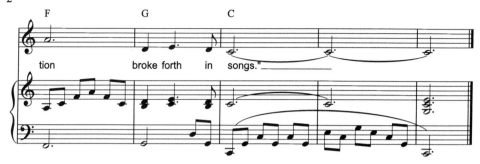

tion      broke forth    in    songs."

1. Hear this Earth mourning deep in pollution,
   Hear this Earth mourning, death in her lungs:
   "How I keep longing for that first morning,
   When all creation broke forth in songs."

2. Hear the trees falling deep in the forest,
   Hear the trees calling, tortured by chain:
   "Where are the song birds, thousands of voices,
   Rising in one symphonic refrain?"

3. Hear the blood crying, crying for justice;
   Hear the blood crying, deep in the ground:
   "Massacres, murders, species forgotten!
   Where is the healing? Where is it found?"

4. Hear the land wailing deep in the darkness,
   Hear the land wailing, crying in pain:
   "Where are my children, torn from their homelands?
   Children, my children, come home again!"

5. Hear that man crying, crucified, dying;
   Hear that man crying, gasping for breath:
   "I'll share your suffering! I'll stop your bleeding!
   I'll bring you healing, even in death!"

# RISE, CREATOR SPIRIT, RISE!

Words: © 1996 Norman Habel

Music: F. Mendelssohn-Bartholdy
adapted W.H. Cummings

# RISE, CREATOR SPIRIT, RISE!

1. Rise, Creator Spirit, rise,
   From this land across the skies.
   Rise from deep within this land,
   Move across the desert sand.
   Rise, create this land anew,
   Make your Dreaming song come true.
   Fill this land with life again;
   Make the desert bloom with rain.
   Fill this land with life again;
   Make the desert bloom with rain.

2. Rise, Creator Spirit, rise,
   From this land across the skies.
   Rise from deep in mystery,
   Rise to set your people free.
   Hear the land cry out in pain,
   Hear her people cry your name.
   Let your rainbow span the Earth
   Giving hope and giving birth.
   Let your rainbow span the Earth
   Giving hope and giving birth.

3. Rise, Creator Spirit, rise,
   From this land across the skies.
   Rise from deep within the tomb,
   Making Jesus' grave a womb.
   Plunging back into your cane,
   Bringing life to ev'ry grave;
   Life that rose with Jesus Christ,
   Rose to fill our heart and eyes.
   Life that rose with Jesus Christ,
   Rose to fill our heart and eyes.

# ONE EARTH

*Words: © 2001 Norman Habel*

*Music: © 2001 Nathaniel Ford*

1.We've on - ly___ one Earth that we can___ call home, One pla - net___ for all life___ to share! With tree frogs, ko - a - las,___ black

2

rhi - nos___ and whales    Still call - ing___ "We hope that___ you

care!"                              We are all con - nect - ed,___

one___ web!___  With ev -'ry life our part - ner,___  one___ breath!

We are all com - mit - ted,__  one___ voice!__   To  cel - e - brate our char - ter, One

# ONE EARTH

1. We've only one Earth that we can call home,
   One planet for all life to share!
   With tree frogs, koalas, black rhinos, and whales
   Still calling, "We hope that you care!"

     We are all connected, one web!
     With ev'ry life our partner, one breath!
     We are all committed, one voice!
     To celebrate our charter,
     One Earth for all to share!

2. It's time to sustain the wonders of Earth
   And not to exploit all her wealth,
   To end all the violence that violates life
   Restore all her arteries to health.

     We are all connected, one web!
     With ev'ry life our partner, one breath!
     We are all committed, one voice!
     To celebrate our charter,
     One Earth for all to share!

3. It's time to honor all peoples on Earth
   Work toward justice for all,
   Indigenous children in tune with the land
   Who suffered colonial rule.

     We are all connected, one web!
     With ev'ry life our partner, one breath!
     We are all committed, one voice!
     To celebrate our charter,
     One Earth for all to share!

4. Our kin on this planet are pleading for us
   To name Earth a true sacred site,
   Revere all the secrets residing within
   And dance her deep dreaming to life.

   We are all connected, one web!
   With ev'ry life our partner, one breath!
   We are all committed, one voice!
   To celebrate our charter,
   One Earth for all to share!

   Come share!
   Come celebrate our charter,
   One Earth for all to share!

   Words: © 2001 Norman Habel

# WONDERFUL

Words: © Norman Habel

Music: © 2001 Douglas Petherick

# CELEBRATE THE LAND

Words: © 1995 Norman Habel

Music: © 1995 Leigh Newton

When the wag-tail tips her tail to God And the kook-a-bur-ra laughs and

laughs a-loud, It's time for all who love the Earth To

cel-e-brate the land, our land, The land who gives us

birth. When the land who feeds our soul.

# CELEBRATE THE LAND

1. When the wagtail tips her tail to God
   And the kookaburra laughs and laughs aloud,
   It's time for all who love this Earth
   To celebrate the land, our land,
   The land who gives us birth.

2. When the stately red gum stands alone
   And the birds of the forest lose their home,
   It's time to fall upon our knees,
   And celebrate the land, our land,
   The land who gives us trees.

3. When the Outback windmill turns to rust
   And the North wind fills the sky with dust,
   It's time to watch for bushfire smoke
   And celebrate the land, our land,
   The land who gives us hope.

4. When the welcome rains have ended drought
   And the seed in the soil begins to sprout,
   It's time for city, country, scrub
   To celebrate the land, our land,
   The land who gives us bread.

5. When the Spirit lifts our eyes to see
   The sacred power in rock and tree,
   Then may a treaty bind us all
   To celebrate the land, our land,
   The land who feeds our soul.

Words: © 1995 Norman Habel

# Part Three

# ADDITIONAL RESOURCES

The following resources may be used throughout the liturgical year or at seasons appropriate to the materials chosen. These materials include invitations to worship, prayers, blessings, reflections, and litanies. Special rites of healing and reconnecting with Earth and sky are suitable for worship in a variety of contexts, including conferences. The Healing Eucharist (p. 197) can be added to a traditional liturgy or incorporated into any of the liturgies in this book. One of the most moving rites is Seven Stations of the Cross (p. 226), a Good Friday rite designed for quiet reflection on the suffering and abuse of our environment. You are invited to use these materials freely at any suitable worship occasion.

# INVITATIONS AND INVOCATIONS

## AN INVITATION FROM EARTH

Take off your shoes.
Like Moses, take off your shoes.
This is holy ground.
Walk gently through my woods.
Tread softly on my face.
Walk reverently through my garden.
This is holy ground.
This is God's sanctuary.

I invite you to worship with your feet this day.
I invite you to walk across my landscape
and sense the life within,
the glory that fills my body—
God's presence below.
I invite you to reach down
to the holy ground beneath you.
Walk in the water.
Sink in the sand.
Stand on a rock.

You are walking on fire,
the fire of God's glory vibrant within.
Take off your shoes.
This is holy ground.
This is the sanctuary of God.

## INVITATION TO CELEBRATE WITH EARTH

Leader      A whisper on the wind,

All      *a song in the night,*

Leader      a call from the deep —

All      *the secret is out:*

Leader      with the dawn once again

All      *Earth will reveal*

Leader      the glory of God

All      *vibrant within.*

Leader      Let Earth rejoice with us!

All      *Let all creation celebrate!*

Leader      Earth is revealed
as the sanctuary of God!
Shalom.

All      *Shalom.*

## AN INDIGENOUS AUSTRALIAN INVITATION

Leader      We invite all our kin in creation
to worship in dance with us:

All      *our sisters shining in the skies,
our ancestors deep within the land,
and kindred spirits yet to be born.*

Leader      We invite the land, our mother,
to worship with us:

All      *ancient gums and saltbush plains,
water holes and sacred caves.*

Leader      We invite the sea to worship with us:

All      *circling sharks and wise old whales,
slippery eels and surfing seals.*

| Leader | We invite our dreamings, our totems, to worship with us: |

*Leader*      We invite our dreamings, our totems,
to worship with us:

*All*      *honey bee and turtle green,*
*platypus, dingo, wallaby.*

*Leader*      We invite our countries to worship with us:

*All*      *our homelands where our spirits dwell,*
*our sacred sites and story lines*
*filled with ancient power.*

*Leader*      We invite you all to be present
as we wait with spirits open
to hear your voices ring
and sing around us.

*All*      *Come, Creator Spirit,*
*stir the voices of creation*
*to join us in celebration.*
*Help us hear them calling*
*as you encircle us*
*with the rainbow of your presence.*

## AN INVOCATION AND A CALL TO REMEMBER

*Voice 1*      Come, Creator,
mother and father of all,
come unite with Earth community,
around the sacred tree of life
and help us remember anew:
the first fresh breath of life,
the first hint of your presence,
the first song in the dawn
that opened our souls to you
and taught us to celebrate.

*Rosemary is a traditional symbol of remembrance. People in the group crush a sprig of rosemary between their fingers and hold up their hands so the aroma fills the air while they make the response below.*

*All*      *Come, help us remember.*

Voice 2        Come, compassionate Christ,
come unite with all creation
around the ancient tree of healing,
and help us remember:
the pains you feel among the suffering poor,
the hurts you feel when Earth is wounded,
the touch of your healing hands —
not only for the few long ago,
but for all creatures on Earth
and for Earth today.

*As before, the sprigs of rosemary are crushed and hands held up to the nose to create and strengthen a sensual memory through the human sense of smell and association.*

All        *Come, help us remember.*

Voice 3        Come, Spirit of life and breath,
come unite with all that inhales
oxygen from the forest trees of life,
and help us remember our breath:
our life from God, the first breath,
our life through the trees of Earth,
our life through the risen Christ,
so that we may become agents of life
as we breathe with all creation.

*As before, the sprigs of rosemary are crushed and hands held up to the nose to create and strengthen a sensual memory through the human sense of smell and association.*

All        *Come, help us remember.*

# RITES OF HEALING AND RECONNECTING

## A RITE OF HEALING

*Worshipers gather round an Earth bowl filled with red clay that is recognized by the group or in the local context as sacred. There are sacred red clays in many cultures, including red ochre in Australia. The color red has symbolic meaning in both the Christian and Jewish faith traditions: it connects us with adam, a biblical Hebrew word that means both red and humanity. It can also be translated as the name "Adam," associated with the first male human being. The worshipers gather round the Earth bowl to share their bond with the soil and to express their bond with Earth.*

*The leader and assistants take the red clay from the center of the Earth bowl and move around the group, marking each of the worshipers with a dab of clay on the ear lobes and below the eyes while repeating the words below. Alternatively, the leader and assistants may move through the whole group without their gathering at the Earth bowl.*

Leader      I invite you to receive the mark of Earth:
to heal your ears
that you may hear the songs of Earth;
to heal your eyes
that you may behold God's presence in Earth.

*On receiving the sacred red clay marks, each person responds with the words below.*

All      *Creator God, bring us home to Earth again,
to hear Earth's voice and see your face.*

*After all have been given the mark of Earth, the leader says the words below to the whole group.*

| | |
|---|---|
| Leader | Receive the mark of Earth<br>on your ears and under your eyes,<br>so you may hear anew the call of Earth<br>and see anew the presence of God<br>in Earth community and its mysteries. |
| All | *Creator God, bring us home to Earth again,*<br>*to hear Earth's voice and see your face*<br>*in all Earth and Earth community.* |
| Leader | Go in peace. Earth welcomes you back into community,<br>to share the healing power of this rite<br>with Earth and with each other. |
| All | *Amen. May it indeed be so. Amen.* |

## A HEALING EUCHARIST

### The Preface

| | |
|---|---|
| Leader | Our God be with you, and with all creation. |
| All | *And also with you.* |
| Leader | Lift up your hearts. |
| All | *We, and all creation,*<br>*lift up our hearts to our God.* |
| Leader | Let us give thanks to our suffering God,<br>our wounded healer. |
| All | *It is right that we give thanks to our God*<br>*who suffers for, and with, us and all creation.* |
| Leader | It is our duty and delight to give thanks<br>to our suffering God, our wounded healer,<br>who made this Earth a sanctuary,<br>and a planet for celebration.<br>This sanctuary, sadly,<br>has become a place of suffering.<br>With all the groaning creation,<br>with our wounded Earth<br>and with the whole community of Earth,<br>we cry out to our God: |

All               *Holy, holy, holy, God of creation,*
*you suffer for Earth and Earth community every day,*
*and daily you share the suffering*
*of Earth and Earth community.*
*Every day you renew your creation, and fill Earth with life.*
*Earth is filled with your glory.*
*We join Earth in praising you.*

## Eucharistic Prayer

Leader      Suffering Creator,
your sanctuary is full of crosses
crosses you still bear:
the cross of timber massacred in rain forests;
the cross of trees cleared without compassion;
the cross of streams polluted with toxins;
the cross of seas poisoned with effluents;
the cross of wild life killed by chemicals;
the cross of lands desecrated by fallout.

You bear these crosses
and suffer the pains in your creation.
And you bring us to the table of life:
here bread and wine
from your sanctuary
are offered to heal creation
and restore hope.

You bear these crosses
and invite us to bear them with you,
and to take up
the crosses in creation with you
and hold them high for all to see.

You bear these crosses,
and invite us to come to the table
to remember how you suffered on the cross.
To bring us forgiveness of our sins —
including our crimes against creation,
to bring healing for the wounds
on the suffering body of Earth,

you came to us as Jesus Christ, the Healer.
On the night when you were betrayed,
you took bread made from the grain of Earth,
and gave thanks.
You broke the bread, and you said:
"Take and eat.
This is my body; I give it to you.
Do this and remember me."

You took the cup of wine —
a blessing from the grapes of Earth —
and you said:
"Take and drink.
This cup is the new covenant sealed in my blood.
Every time you drink from this cup, remember me."

I am asking you to remember today,
every time you eat this bread
and drink this wine at God's table,
that you are invited to share the cross
of your suffering Creator —
the wounded healer of all creation —
so that the healing power of Jesus Christ's body and blood
may heal you and also, through you,
the illnesses and pains of Earth and all creation.

## Agnus Dei (Lamb of God)

All
*Suffering healer,*
*who takes away our sins*
*against your sanctuary,*
*have mercy on us*
*and heal us,*
*and heal our planet.*
*Suffering creature,*
*who takes away our sins*
*against creation,*
*have mercy on us*
*and heal us,*
*and heal our planet.*

*Suffering Lamb of God, Jesus Christ,*
*who takes away our sins*
*against Earth,*
*grant your peace to us*
*and to our planet.*
*Amen.*

Leader        Come to God's table.
Everything is ready.
Come and participate in the healing meal
with all God's creation.
Come and be healed;
come and receive God's peace.

*The leader and assistants distribute the Eucharist according to the usual custom of the worshiping group.*

## Blessing

*The blessing may be proclaimed to the group by the leader or be said by the group to each other, in unison.*

Leader        May the life-giving power
of Jesus Christ's body and blood
flow through your veins,
flow through your lives,
and flow through this Earth.
May this life-giving power
bring healing and hope
wherever there are wounds,
and brokenness.
Go in peace,
and serve your God,
each other,
and all creation.
Amen.

# RITE FOR RECONNECTING WITH EARTH

*This ritual is designed to help us reconnect with Earth as our spiritual source of life and uses a bowl filled with Earth to symbolize Earth itself.*

*An earthen bowl, standing on a pedestal and filled with earth — the Earth bowl — is placed in the center of the worship space. At the center of the Earth bowl is a single lighted candle — the Earth candle — representing Earth's soul.*

*Participants are invited to gather round the Earth bowl in four small groups. Each participant holds a small candle. Each group represents and is aligned with one of the four chief directions of the Western compass: north, south, east, and west. To aid participants, these compass directions may be marked on the floor at the base of the Earth bowl pedestal.*

## Cry for Connection

*The leader, facing each group in turn — east, south, west, north — asks the same question. Each group responds in turn, as it is addressed. This ritual is repeated until every person in the worshiping group is holding a lighted candle.*

| | |
|---|---|
| Leader | How can we connect again with the soul of Earth, the damaged, suffering, and resisting soul of Earth? |
| East Group | How can we connect again with the soul of Earth, the deep waters, the deep deep below, the waters from which we emerged, the womb from which life was born? How can we connect again with the soul of Earth, the forgotten voice we heard in the womb, the song that gave us life and voice? |

*At the end of the statement, each person in the group aligned to the east lights an individual candle from the Earth candle. The leader turns to the south.*

| | |
|---|---|
| Leader | How can we connect again with the soul of Earth, the damaged, suffering, and resisting soul of Earth? |
| South Group | How can we connect again with the soul of Earth, lands abused and lands made bare, lands that sustain the wide web of life and offer all creatures Earth's rich care? |

How can we connect again with the land,
whose spirit and soul are known
to the Indigenous peoples who live close to Earth,
are kin with the soil?

*At the end of the statement, each person in the group aligned to the south lights an individual candle from the Earth candle. The leader turns to the west.*

Leader      How can we connect again with the soul of Earth,
the damaged, suffering, and resisting soul of Earth?

West Group  How can we connect again with the soul of Earth,
a suffering soul suppressed by minds
of economic rationalists —
minds that convinced us there is no soul,
no spirit that animates matter,
only the sounds in our mind?
How can we connect with the soul of Earth:
a voice we have tried to ignore?
a parent who nurtures our life?
a lover who longs for partnership?

*At the end of the statement, each person in the group aligned to the west lights an individual candle from the Earth candle. The leader turns to the north.*

Leader      How can we connect again with the soul of Earth,
the damaged, suffering, and resisting soul of Earth?

North Group  How can we connect again with the soul of Earth,
the soul of Earth who refuses to die,
though terrorized by human greed and lust.—
crimes against creation and life?
How can we connect again with Earth
who has sacrificed so much for us,
has been damaged at our hands,
and still invites us all to come back home
and celebrates with us renewal and life?

*At the end of the statement, each person in the group aligned to the north lights an individual candle from the Earth candle. The leader turns slowly in a circle, addressing all groups.*

Leader       Earth gives us life and sustains us.
Earth nurtures our life
even when we have returned death for life.
Today Earth invites us to accept her offer,
to link again with Earth's songs of life,
to link again with the soul of Earth,
to hear again the voice of God.

All       *Earth, we are sorry.*
*Earth, please forgive us.*
*Help us sustain you*
*as you have sustained us:*
*nurturing our bodies and giving us life.*

## Commitment: Promise the Earth

All       *God, Creator Spirit, and suffering healer,*
*we, the children of Earth*
*recognize that we have exploited Earth.*
*From now on*
*we promise Earth*
*that we will respect all Earth's life-forms,*
*and celebrate them*
*as valued members of Earth community.*
*We promise Earth*
*that we will care for Earth*
*as Earth cares for us,*
*protect the Earth community from harm,*
*and preserve Earth's resources so that future generations*
*will have healthy food, pure air and water, and fertile soil*
*in order to live full lives.*
*We promise Earth*
*that we will struggle to overcome forces and powers*
*that keep members of Earth community*
*poor, oppressed, and excluded.*

> *We promise Earth*
> *that we will use Earth's resources to sustain life*
> *rather than exploit it.*
> *Yes, we promise the Earth!*

*At the end of the ritual of commitment, the participants each move forward and place their candles in the Earth bowl. If the worshiping group is large, there may need to be extra trays of soil placed around the Earth bowl.*

Leader      May this promise you have made,
            this ritual of connection with Earth,
            bind you to Earth again
            in a deep and spiritual way.
            Go in peace.
            And serve Earth.
            Amen.

## RITES FOR RECONNECTING WITH SKY

### Suggested Ritual Activities

*You may choose to use any or all of these activities as you design a rite for reconnecting with sky.*

• During an initial song or the Invitation to Worship, ribbon banners, windsocks, decorative flags, or Chinese kites may be carried into the worship space on long poles so they can be waved above the group. If these processional items are placed in a stationary location within the worship area, electric fans — located appropriately and placed unobtrusively — may be used to keep the items moving during the service of worship.

• Lengths of ribbon or unbleached muslin strips can be made available for each person in the worship group. During the general prayers or meditation period, the participants each hold a ribbon while they pray or meditate; these ribbons can later be used as prayer ribbons — similar to Buddhist prayer flags — to symbolize that our prayers and meditations are being carried by the winds through sky to the Creator God. Some may choose to write their prayer and meditation thoughts on the ribbon prior to tying it where it can blow in the wind. The prayer ribbons can be tied to a tree branch in the church area for a period of time, or left until nature reclaims them. Alternatively, individuals may take their ribbons away with them and tie them somewhere they can blow in the wind: in their garden or in a local park (it may be wise to check with the local council or government authority before tying prayer and meditation ribbons in public places).

• The sounds of gongs, temple bells, or singing bowls — all emitting sounds carried by air — can be used to call worshipers to prayer and meditation; the sounds can also symbolize that prayers and meditations are carried by air to God. A gong or bell struck repeatedly or a singing bowl may be carried through a gathered worship group to assist people into a state of focused prayerful meditation. A gong, bell, or singing bowl may also be sounded after prayers or prayer petitions or at the end of a period of meditation.

• A large feather (if possible, taken from a white turkey), with a length of ribbon, yarn, or string tied to it, is passed around the assembly. As the participants each hold the feather, they voice their prayer silently or aloud and then pass the feather to the next person. If the group is large, it may be appropriate to use several feathers. At the conclusion of the prayers, the feather is tied to a tree branch or bush outside as a reminder of our prayers; it can remain outside until nature claims it.

• Worshipers of all ages may engage together in kite flying, cloud gazing, or star watching; these activities celebrate the wonder of air and sky.

NOTE: *the following ritual activities, though well-intentioned and spectacular, should be avoided because of the harm they cause to Earth and members of Earth community:*

• Avoid the release of helium balloons. They are detrimental to the environment, especially to marine life.

• Avoid the release of butterflies. Most butterflies are raised in commercial conditions for the single purpose of "ritual release." Even with precise timing and ideal weather conditions, many of the butterflies will not survive more than a few minutes.

• Avoid the release of doves since most are not raised to survive in the wild.

# *TAPETE:* SAWDUST PAINTING
# AND RITUAL DANCE FOR EARTH[1]

## Context

A *Tapete* is a carpet of "painted" sawdust and comes from the cultural traditions of Brazil and Guatemala, where it is used during religious and community celebrations. The sawdust is hand-dyed in the colors required for each design. The design is chosen because of its symbolic meaning for the group participating in the ritual.

*Tapete* is an impermanent art form, and as such it is a suitable symbolic ritual for celebrating the changing seasons of Earth: birth, death, rebirth, and return to creation. In a *Tapete* celebration, people dance or walk through the sawdust design and destroy the design in the process. This "transformation through celebration" is an integral part of a *Tapete:* a ritual or dance act symbolizing the impermanence and transitions inherent in the life cycles of Earth and Earth community.

Both artists and members of the worshiping group may find the prospect of destroying the lovely work of group art and faith unsettling: it seems too beautiful to destroy! But the sensation of walking and dancing through the sawdust barefoot or in socks is a profoundly connective one: participants can experience the design's life, death, rebirth as an art form, and return to chaos. It is cathartic and spiritually satisfying to follow the life cycle through all its changes. And in Earth community *Tapete* celebrations, sawdust too praises life and dances!

## Background

The art students in the Creation Theology Group of Newton, Massachusetts, chose a tree of life design for their liturgical *Tapete* painting. The design, ten feet x ten feet (about three meters x three meters), was drawn on large sheets of paper.

## Preparation for Using a *Tapete* in a Group Celebration

*Before the Celebration*

1. Select and create a design that is large enough for the anticipated space and number of people.

---

1. These directions were composed and crafted by artist and religious educator Nita Penfold. Nita learned the techniques for creating the *Tapete* from Jennifer Hereth at the University of Creation Spirituality in Oakland, California.

Additional Resources

2. Transfer the design to a paper template. Tape the design to a larger sheet of plastic if the *Tapete* is to be performed indoors. Decide on the colors to be used in the finished design.

3. Obtain sawdust, suitable water-based pigment, and garbage bags or an alternative convenient container for mixing sawdust and paint and storing sawdust prior to the celebration.[2]

4. At least one day prior to the celebration, dye the sawdust with the water-based pigments. The dyed mixture should feel like crumbly biscuit dough. This step may take several hours.

5. Allow the sawdust to dry, which may also take several hours. The sawdust should feel dry to the touch when it is used in a *Tapete* design.[3]

*On the Day of the Celebration*

1. Lay out the template in the worship space.

2. Starting at the center of the design and working to the outside, fill in the design creating a "carpet" of sawdust two to four inches (five to ten centimeters) deep.

3. Take photos of the artists at work on the design and at the completion of the design.

4. As necessary, comfort artists, dancers, and liturgists; encourage participants to enjoy the physicality of the dance and to weep and rejoice in the celebration of the "birth, death, rebirth, and return to creation" of the design — a symbolic celebration of the cycles of life in Earth community.

_____

2. Care must be taken in procuring sawdust, since some building materials are treated with arsenic. Ask your lumber yard or home improvement store for sawdust from "virgin" wood (not treated with any toxic chemicals). Those with respiratory ailments may wish to wear simple dust-masks during the dying procedure to avoid any exposure to dust. Any kind of pigment may be used as long as it is water-based: latex house paint, tempera paint, artist acrylic paints. If the design requires large amounts of sawdust to be dyed, we recommend using house paint — the cheapest pigment — because a great deal of pigment is needed. The sawdust absorbs the pigment and water and feels dry to the touch when it is ready to use for the design. It will go through a stage in the drying process where it looks and feels a bit like crumbly tortilla or biscuit dough. We recommend one part pigment to three parts water. Add the pigment mixed with water to the sawdust bit by bit and knead until the whole batch of sawdust is evenly colored.

3. Dancing or moving on wet sawdust can be dangerous; it is advisable to ensure the sawdust is dry to the touch before using it in a *Tapete* celebration, and to use music with a slow rhythm. Also, it is wise to advise participants to move at a speed and in a style with which they feel both safe and comfortable; there is no need to celebrate a *Tapete* with fast or complex movements, so people of any age group, with varying degrees of mobility and with varying levels of fitness, can be part of the spiral dance.

# EARTH LITURGY:
# A "DANCE FOR THE EARTH" SEQUENCE[4]

## Why a *Tapete?*

One of the key symbolic actions in a *Tapete* is that people walking or dancing through the sawdust return the dust to dust. Moving over the sawdust with bare feet feels just wonderful, so invite people to remove their socks; it may be a good idea to let people know that they will be invited to participate in a "bare feet" activity prior to the *Tapete* celebration so they can come prepared! If people do not remove their socks, the socks may be stained by the dye used to color the sawdust.

The *Tapete* is grounded in the philosophy that humans are a cog — one of many — in the cosmic wheel of life. How do we help each other understand and experience this perspective? We can dance a *Tapete*. There are very simple dances that include walking in lines. The group involved in the celebration joins hands in a broken circle. A leader moves the circle into a spiral as they move through the *Tapete* design. Each person is a necessary part of the circle, but the performance of a *Tapete* is not really about individual expression; rather, a *Tapete* celebration encourages participants to each experience themselves as a part of something larger than themselves. All human beings are part of the ecosystem, and in a *Tapete* celebration people participate in this experience of interconnection with creation — both by dancing together, and by destroying/recreating the sawdust picture. In Earth community, as in the *Tapete*, each individual plays a role in the bigger "dance" of creation.

## Music

Any piece of music can be used, though music with a slower rhythm and slower speed is recommended.[5]

## Children

Children can be included in the *Tapete* celebration in several ways. Young children can be held, or they can hold hands and be part of the spiral. Because many paints available and commonly used in Western industrial

---

4. Composed and created by Marilyn Richards, folk dance instructor, Physical Education Department, Massachusetts Institute of Technology (Cambridge, Massachusetts).

5. At the original performance of this liturgical celebration, the group chose the song "Listen," from the album *Listen*, written by the Monks of the Weston Priory (Weston, Vermont).

Additional Resources

societies are dangerous when ingested, it is not recommended that children be left to play in the center of the *Tapete,* as is the practice in some *Tapete* traditions.

## Dance Movement

Ask the group to form a circle around the sawdust painting. Invite the participants to hold hands[6] with the people next to them to form a linked chain of people.

If sheet music is to be used, ask people to line up, in approximate order of height, one behind the other, with their right hand resting on the right shoulder of the person in front of them. The sheet of music or words can be held in place with the right hand, which is a comfortable reading distance for many people.

The dance leader and assistants decide on the best dance movement to ensure everyone in the line is standing on the sawdust design at the end of the dance.

The types of movement chosen may depend on the ages of the participants. Skipping and walking in time to the music are options for groups that include diverse ages. The purpose of a *Tapete* is to be together, be part of the celebration, feel the sawdust under the feet; it is not a dance performance!

Alternatively, the dance can be choreographed as follows: take a step with the right foot, swing the left foot across the sawdust. Then take a step with the left foot and swing the right foot across the sawdust to break up the picture. Repeat in time to the music until the picture is broken up. (The dance leader and assistants may need to demonstrate the movement; some people learn movement through watching and doing.)

## Speed

A slower speed is most convenient for all ages, and is less likely to result in people slipping and falling.

## Pattern

Two patterns can be used to move the group onto the picture: a spiral, with the line circling into the center, or a snake-like zigzag from one side to the other. The spiral works for smaller groups, the snake for larger groups.

---

6. A standard accepted in some cultures is palm up for the right hand, palm down for the left hand.

In both cases, the line moves slowly onto the design, and people move close beside others until the whole design space is covered by people's feet. Regardless of the movement chosen, the aim is to have the whole group on the image at the same time, moving rhythmically to produce a chaotic multicolored pattern.

## Ending the Dance

When everyone in the group has moved onto the design, the dance leader calls "stop."

## Things You Can Do at the End of a *Tapete*

- Say a prayer. A worship leader or a group member can compose a prayer; anyone in the group can be invited to add a petition to a group prayer; everyone can be invited to pray or meditate for a few minutes in silence.

- Invite the participants to put their hands on the shoulders of the person next to them in a group hug.

- Encourage people to enjoy the experience, to talk to and celebrate with each other: to make a joyful noise and enjoy the shared experience.

- Encourage people to focus on their experiences: the sawdust under their feet and between their toes; the closeness with other people; moving rhythmically with a whole group of people. Give people time to process their experiences. Invite people to share their feelings and experiences.

- Allow people to feel free to move off the design. Some people will find the closeness wonderful; for others it will be difficult because people are too close. Differences in interpersonal comfort are personal and cultural.

- Sing a song focusing on group solidarity, such as "They'll Know We Are Christians by Our Love."

- Invite people to "Go in peace to love and serve Earth!"

# LITANIES

## A LITANY OF THE CREATING WORD

Leader    In the beginning was the Word, waiting,
resting, suspended in timeless time.

All    *And God said, "Good. How very good!"*

Leader    And the Word gathered from within itself
endless energies to create the first burst of light,
the beginning of life.

All    *And God said, "Good. How very good!"*

Leader    And the Word expanded itself
with boundless leaps of time to create space,
where the emerging cosmos could be.

All    *And God said, "Good. How very good."*

Leader    And the Word took one fragment of cosmic matter
to form a chosen planet,
a blue-green ball of life called Earth.

All    *And God said, "Good. How very good!"*

Leader    And the Word set this precious planet
in a solar system within a gaping galaxy
filled with mystery.

All    *And God said, "Good. How very good!"*

Leader    And the Word spun a web,
an infinite maze of immense, intricate life-forms:
a living cell system to match the solar system.

All    *And God said, "Good. How very good."*

| | |
|---|---|
| Leader | And the Word multiplied the life within itself<br>to form a frenzy of living species,<br>each linked to each other for survival. |
| All | *And God said, "Good. How very good."* |
| Leader | And the Word created human beings<br>to be an expression of itself among all species,<br>and speak the message of life. |
| All | *And God said, "Good. How very good."* |
| Leader | And the Word rested, present in all creation,<br>waiting for human beings to hear the Word<br>and keep the planet alive. |

## A LITANY OF THE CREATING WISDOM

| | |
|---|---|
| Leader | In the beginning was Wisdom, waiting,<br>resting, suspended in timeless time. |
| All | *And God said, "Good. How very good!"* |
| Leader | And Wisdom gathered from within itself<br>endless energies to create the first burst of light,<br>the beginning of life. |
| All | *And God said, "Good. How very good!"* |
| Leader | And Wisdom expanded itself<br>with boundless leaps of time to create space,<br>where the emerging cosmos could be. |
| All | *And God said, "Good. How very good."* |
| Leader | And Wisdom took one fragment of cosmic matter<br>to form a chosen planet,<br>a blue-green ball of life called Earth. |
| All | *And God said, "Good. How very good!"* |
| Leader | And Wisdom set this precious planet<br>in a solar system within a gaping galaxy<br>filled with mystery. |
| All | *And God said, "Good. How very good!"* |

Leader
And Wisdom spun a web,
an infinite maze of immense intricate life-forms:
a living cell system to match the solar system.

All
*And God said, "Good. How very good."*

Leader
And Wisdom multiplied the life within itself
to form a frenzy of living species,
each linked to each other for survival.

All
*And God said, "Good. How very good."*

Leader
And Wisdom created human beings
to be an expression of itself among all species,
and speak the message of life.

All
*And God said, "Good. How very good."*

Leader
And Wisdom rested, present in all creation,
waiting for human beings to hear Wisdom's voice
and keep the planet alive.

## LITANY OF PRAISE
## (adapted from Psalm 148)

All
*Blessed are you, God of Earth and sky.*
*Through your holy breath you give life to all creation.*

Leader
Praise God from sky.
Praise God from the heights above.
Praise God: all you divine messengers and heavenly hosts.
Praise God: sun and moon, all you shining stars.
You, highest heavens and you, waters above sky:
Praise God.

All
*Blessed are you, God of Earth and sky.*
*Through your holy breath you give life to all creation.*

Leader
Let everything praise the name of God,
for God commanded and they were created.
God set them in place forever and ever,
and gave them a duty that will not pass away.

| | |
|---|---|
| All | *Blessed are you, God of Earth and sky.* |
| | *Through your holy breath you give life to all creation.* |
| Leader | Praise God from Earth: |
| | you great sea creatures and all ocean depths; |
| | lightning and hail, snow and clouds; |
| | stormy winds that do God's bidding; |
| | you mountains and all hills, fruit trees and all cedars; |
| | wild animals and all cattle, |
| | small creatures and flying birds. |
| All | *Blessed are you, God of Earth and sky.* |
| | *Through your holy breath you give life to all creation.* |
| Leader | Let the rulers of Earth and all peoples, |
| | young men and maidens, old folks and children, |
| | praise the name of God, |
| | for that name alone is to be exalted. |
| | Let all that breathes and exists give glory to God. |
| | May the winds carry the praise of all God's people. |
| All | *Blessed are you, God of Earth and sky.* |
| | *Through your holy breath you give life to all creation.* |

# PRAYERS

## A NESW PRAYER[1]
(based on Native American Tradition)

Leader     O God, you graciously encompass us
with your care as we live on Earth,
a planet traveling through your sky.
Inspire us from every direction —
north, east, south, and west —
with your life-giving Spirit,
that we may faithfully serve you on all our pathways.
We ask this in the name of Jesus the anointed one.

All     *Let north, east, south, and west cry, "Amen!"*

## PSALM 23
(an Indigenous prayer developed by the Rainbow Spirit Elders in
northeastern Australia)

The Creator is my Elder,
I shall not want.

My Elder guides me through the bush
to where food is plentiful,
finds sacred water holes for me,
strengthens my spirit,
and leads me in the right tracks
according to the law of the bush.

Even though I walk
where the land has been desecrated
by white invaders,

---

1. A north, east, south, west prayer.

I fear no foreign power;
your presence and your Spirit comfort me.

You join us around the campfire when we sing
in the presence of our oppressors.

You fill us with your Spirit when we dance
and make our ceremonies strong.

Surely our lives are always
filled with good things from our mother, the land;
and we will live with you forever,
here in this sacred place,
where you dwell deep deep within.

## A PRAYER BASED ON PSALM 104

Leader     Let us pray.
O God, you are very great;
you are clothed with splendor and majesty.
You stretch out sky like a tent,
make the clouds your chariot,
and ride on the wings of the wind.
The breezes are your messengers.
May your breath blow across our hearts,
filling us with deep wisdom, hope, love,
and the desire for justice,
as we continue our journey
upon your Earth and through your sky.

We ask this in the name of Jesus,
the breath of life for us.

_All_        _Amen._

## A PRAYER FOR GOD'S BREATH

Leader     God our great potter,
remember that first morning and
breathe again your moist breath:
on the dust of Earth,

on the wastelands of our planet,
on the barren wilderness,
and mold new wombs for life,
fragile forms that fly,
and living creatures that dream
of tomorrow
when the groaning of creation ceases,
and the desert breaks forth again in song.
Shalom.

All          *Shalom.*

# BLESSINGS

## BLESSING OF EARTH

Leader    In the breath of dawn
may you know the sensation
of kookaburras[1] repeating
the original oration
when the morning stars sang
at the birth of Earth.

In the fire of noon
may you feel the pain
of Jesus Christ in the poor
who have no land,
no Earth to inherit,
no home.

In the dusk of day
may you find the peace
of Earth at rest
while grains swell
ready to rise with Christ
in the dawn.

All    *In the dawn,*
*in the heat,*
*in the dusk*
*we will celebrate birth amid death in planet Earth.*

Leader    May the Earth be healing for you.

All    *And also for you.*

---

1. The kookaburra is a sign of good news among Indigenous Australian groups: it announces and celebrates the dawn with laughter. An explanation for this understanding of the role of the kookaburra in some Indigenous communities is included after the Kookaburra Blessing on p. 222.

| Leader | Go in peace! Serve Earth! |
|--------|---------------------------|
| *All*  | *Amen.*                   |

## A SHALOM BLESSING

May you feel the force of shalom
unleashing life in the morning,
a surge of strength through the day
and the peace of God at night.

May the blue of the skies
open your eyes
and the song of shalom
carry you home
to the sacred sites of Earth.

## A SPIRIT BLESSING

May the Spirit surprise you
like a dove from above,
or a swallow from below,
but now and then as a blue wren.

## A DAWN BLESSING

May the Spirit in the dawn
open your eyes to see
the shadow of God
move barely visible
like brolgas:
graceful blue-gray birds,
sliding through the ghost gums
and
portending the presence
that brings all into being
with the dawn.

## A LOVE BLESSING
(for weddings)

May the God who creates the soft wings of butterflies,
the God who glides by gently as black swans,
the God whose warm word opens wildflowers,
create within each of you
the will to hold each other softly,
the love to invade each other gently,
the word to speak with one another warmly.

May the God who is the hidden music in each conception,
the God who is midwife through the pains of birth,
the God whose Spirit blows in the first breath we take,
bind you together
to bring forth something new within each of you,
to nurture your pains with compassion,
to explore the mystery of the spirit between you.

May the Jesus Christ who walked incognito to Emmaus,
the Jesus who revealed his presence in a quiet meal,
the Christ who was risen and free for eyes of faith to see,
be present with you in your love,
walking quietly with you along the way,
making every meal a surprise, a picnic of faith,
revealing himself as risen and real at his sacred table
in your house and your landscape.

## AUSSIE BLESSINGS

May there always be echidnas,
anteaters at the bottom of your garden,
so that ants never get up your nose.

May the God who made kangaroos with long tails,
emus with long necks
and lives with long endings
keep your troubles short, sharp, and shiny.

May white ants never live in your foundations,
mice never live in your bread bin,
nor possums ever live — or die — in your ceiling,
but instead, may they roam free.

May the gentle spin
of the blue wren
make you stress
less.

## A BLESSING FOR EARTH IN PAIN

Beloved Earth,
may the God who grieves and grieves
over the injustice which crushes the weak,
may the God who struggled with Job
and felt the barbs of his anguish,
may the God who heard a son cry from the cross
and felt his feeling of forsaken presence —
yes, may the God who experienced Golgotha,
and Auschwitz and Indigenous massacres,
and children torn from their cultures,
share your pain,
share you loss,
share your struggle,
share the memory of loving trust betrayed by
humans,
share your cross,
and share the hope that you will be loved again
by the human custodians
entrusted with your care.

## BLESSINGS FROM INDIA

May God, the mother of the village well
and the village women,
help you draw water for life
and laughter.

May God, the father of the outcaste poor
and deserted Dalits, the untouchables,
meet you waiting in their streets
and teach you hope.

May Jesus, a son to malnourished mothers
and a brother to unwanted daughters,
teach you to be a midwife who brings new life
from the risen one.

May the Spirit who seeks justice for Earth oppressed
by the ways of the past,
lead you to open your eyes
to see the path beyond evil to freedom.

May Jesus Christ, the poor one,
Jesus Christ, the malnourished one,
Jesus Christ, the suffering one,
Jesus Christ, the Earth one,
Jesus Christ, the Dalit,
Jesus Christ, the Tribal,
look up from the dusty ground
and make his face shine on you.

## A KOOKABURRA BLESSING

May the laugh of the kookaburra[2]
echo through the hills
to announce the dawn,
and the good news
that Jesus Christ has come
to turn our sadness into laughter,
our suffering Earth
into a vibrant singing planet.

Laugh, Kookaburra, Laugh!

---

2. Note: the kookaburra is a sign of good news among Indigenous Australian groups: it announces and celebrates the dawn with laughter.

*Why is the kookaburra the symbol of good news for some Aboriginal peoples of far northern Queensland? Because the kookaburra announces the sunrise, the dawning of a new day! There is a traditional Dreaming story behind this belief. The story, as told to Norman Habel by the Rainbow Spirit Elders, is as follows.*

*In the beginning, the elders met to choose the bird who would sing their ceremonies. They needed a bird with a powerful and beautiful voice to sing ceremony strong. They first invited Parrot to sing. But Parrot's voice was too sharp and piercing. Next they invited Mopoke, but his voice was too deep and unhappy. Then they invited Cockatoo, but her voice screeched too much. Finally they invited Kookaburra to sing. Kookaburra's voice was rich, strong and cheerful. So Kookaburra was chosen to announce the dawn and sing the ceremonies. So now you will hear the Kookaburra singing at dawn in the bush. And if Kookaburra sings during the day it is the good news that someone important is coming. And that is why some Aboriginal Christians say Kookaburra is also a symbol of the Gospel, the Good News from God that someone important is coming each Christmas and every day.*

# MISSION STATEMENT

## OUR MISSION TO CREATION

**We, who know the love of the Creator through the cross of Jesus Christ, are called:**

to honor Earth as one sacred site in all the cosmos
where God has chosen to dwell in person
and which God has chosen to fill with God's glory and presence;

to explore creation as a web of intricate living relationships
held together by the wisdom of God
in a mysterious rhythm called life;

to love Earth completely as God did by sending an only son
to be united forever with one piece of Earth called Jesus
so that all things in Earth might be reconciled to God;

to oppose those destructive powers on Earth
that plunder the limited resources of this planet for profit
and that take food from the poor of the world
to feed the greed of the rich;

to suffer with our ailing Earth,
to listen with compassion to the cries of Earth—
from its forests, its rivers, its farmlands, and its atmosphere—
in their struggle against the forces of death;

to celebrate the hope of Earth
as it resists the poisons that threaten its life,
recovers from nuclear explosions and deforestation
and longs for final liberation from bondage;

to care for Earth as an intimate community of companions
who are dependent on each other for survival
and who are to be treasured as kin—

224

rather than be dominated or be used as mere things,
or be regarded as objects
who have no rights to flourish
and be fulfilled as themselves,
and be respected because
they are the beloved creations of God.

# STATIONS OF THE CROSS

## THE SEVEN STATIONS MODEL

### Context

Good Friday has traditionally been the time when we remember the journey of Jesus Christ to his crucifixion on Calvary. The traditional Christian ritual known as the "stations of the cross" reminds us of places and moments of Jesus' suffering along the way on the journey to the cross and his death.

In many countries across the planet, there are people suffering because of the way they and the environment have been abused. There are also places of suffering: locations where evil acts have been committed — both against the land and the peoples of the land, and against people at that place.

This liturgical ritual provides a model for a seven stations liturgy exploring places associated with suffering and abuse in the local community; it uses the Christian understanding of Jesus' suffering for all creation as a way of enriching our response to the suffering and abuse that is part of our local history. In this model a series of places is identified in the worshiping group's country or local community where individuals, groups of people, or Earth have suffered or been abused. As Christians, we are called to acknowledge this suffering and abuse. We recognize that Jesus Christ also calls us to walk with our God in these places and demonstrate our regret and pain by what we say and what we do both ritually and in our lives outside the celebration of the liturgical ritual.

### Using the Seven Stations Liturgy Model

The seven stations model may be used in several ways, depending on the local context. The groups involved in the celebration of the seven stations should decide whether the focus will be exclusively on the sufferings and abuse of the environment or whether the liturgy will also embrace places where crimes were committed against Indigenous people or other inno-cent people. A worshiping community could celebrate the whole liturgy at seven places of abuse and suffering in their local community. Or wor-shiping communities in each region of a larger location (a region, state, or country) could name a local place of abuse and suffering in their re-gion, and this location would be named in the liturgy as one of the seven stations named in each local community's celebration of the liturgy. If possible, the local community should celebrate at the station of abuse and suffering in their region; however, this may not always be feasible.

In addition, these liturgical celebrations of the seven stations could be held simultaneously around the country at local stations of abuse and suf-fering. Symbolically, they would demonstrate seven stations of suffering in joint worship across a country or local community, with the whole liturgy celebrated at each of the seven stations identified in the larger region. As such, these individual and scattered celebrations are a community of worshipers — a body of Christ — suffering and remembering suffering in solidarity with each other, with Earth community, and with Jesus Christ, our "God with us," who became a piece of Earth, a piece of matter, for and with us and all creation.

The following outline offers a model for a seven stations liturgy. Each station identified as a place of abuse and suffering is linked to one of the seven words of Jesus from the cross.

STATION 1: a place where a people (genocide) or a forest has died.

STATION 2: a place where species have died.

STATION 3: a place made desolate by a nuclear disaster or atomic fallout.

STATION 4: a place made desolate by salt or waste.

STATION 5: a place polluted by chemicals and toxins.

STATION 6: a place where air pollution kills people or plants or animals.

STATION 7: the crucified land.

The following seven stations liturgy uses this model to identify with the seven stations of abuse and suffering in an Australian context.

Worshipers may wish to pause after the readings at each station to reflect on the events and the place the station represents. At each station it is also appropriate to sing softly a verse of "Hear This Earth Mourning" (p. 178), returning to verse 1 at station 6.

## STATIONS UNDER THE SOUTHERN CROSS:
### A Good Friday Liturgy[1]

| | |
|---|---|
| STATION 1 | The Island of Genocide |
| WORD 1 | "It is finished" (John 19:30–37) |
| Leader | We begin our journey on the island of genocide, the island known to us as Tasmania. We walk across the island, as the early settlers did, in that long killing line that sought to erase the "savages." "It is finished!" they cried. "The black line has done its job!"[2] There are no mounds or markers, no names from the Aboriginal nation massacred. There are no people mourning, no heroes remembered for their bravery. There are no bloodstains. Yet from Earth their blood still cries, cries for the land, cries for justice, remembrance, and rest. In the going down of the sun and in the morning will we remember them? |
| All | *God, in your mercy, help us remember them.* |
| STATION 2 | To an Unknown Species |
| WORD 2 | "Into your hands I commend my spirit" (Luke 23:44–49) |
| Leader | We come to a bare hillside, a blank space where once timbers stood: tall testimonies to time. |

---

1. This liturgy could also be used in the Season of Lent.
2. "The black line" is the line of armed settlers that stretched single file across the island of Tasmania and marched through the island to exterminate all blacks.

We ask about the species that once lived there:
the Tasmanian tiger and the tree frog
and a thousand unknown species
that are no more.
Shall we erect a monument
to the unknown species
who gave their lives that we might have wood
for nothing more than paper?
Shall we cry aloud,
"Into your hands we commend their spirits" —
and then forget our animal kin existed?

All

*God, in your mercy,*
*help us remember.*

STATION 3

Maralinga Sites

WORD 3

"Why have you forsaken me?" (Matthew 27:45–54)

Leader

We stand before the dry reaches of Maralinga,
desolate and desecrated.
We cross the broken fence that warns
of radioactive fallout still living
long after the atomic blasts of the fifties.
We meet a few Indigenous people
returning to the fringes of bomb sites
that once were sacred sites.
And we ask them whether their suffering
from the fallout, their forced removal,
and the desecration of their lands,
was worth the sacrifice.
"After all," said the politicians,
"we need to test these bombs
to keep the free world free."
And can we hear the ground crying,
the land wailing,
Earth screaming,
"Why have you forsaken me?"

All

*God, in your mercy,*
*help us remember them.*

| | |
|---|---|
| STATION 4 | Pillars of Salt |
| WORD 4 | "I thirst" (John 19:28–29) |
| Leader | Far across the farmlands of the west |

we meet the rising salt.
Cropping to excess without concern for the future
has led to increased salinity.
The soil dies, the salt rises — and we move on
to clear another stretch of virgin land.
Shall we erect pillars of salt
on each farm where we have polluted the soil
as a reminder that the land is God's
and we are its custodians
for the future?
Shall we pause to hear the hoarse whispers
of grasses, lizards, camels:
"I thirst! I die!"

| | |
|---|---|
| All | *God, in your mercy,*<br>*help us remember them.* |
| STATION 5 | Solomon's Mines |
| WORD 5 | "Today you will be with me in paradise" (Luke 23:39–43) |
| Leader | We pause now before a massive mine, |

the mark of progress by an international company.
We behold Ok Tedi, on a hill of Papua New Guinea,
the pinnacle of our mining prowess!
And we look downstream from what once was paradise,
from the mine
where the waste has been flushed,
supposedly washed away into the sea.
But the waste lives on like death
along the sides of the river.
No life can be sustained,
no villages survive —
only a wilderness of waste.
Shall we ignore these mining disasters
as simply the price of progress?

|  |  |
|---|---|
|  | Or will we learn from Solomon<br>that wisdom is more than wealth?<br>Can we promise those who die in the tropics,<br>"Today you will be with me in paradise?" |
| All | *God, in your mercy,*<br>*help us remember.* |
| STATION 6 | Castles in the Air |
| WORD 6 | "Father, forgive them" (Luke 23:32–34) |
| Leader | As we reach a big industrial city,<br>we smell the fumes in the air,<br>we see the chemicals in the atmosphere,<br>we feel the UV rays.<br>"Fossil fuel," we cry, "is still the only way<br>to build our castles in the air,<br>to keep the economy ever increasing."<br>Instead of castles we have carbons in the air;<br>instead of a shelter we have ozone holes;<br>instead of wisdom we have greenhouse warnings.<br>Do we have the will to clean God's air<br>and go slow?<br>Or will we harness a new power<br>and learn to go even faster?<br>Can we hear a voice from the cross,<br>"Father, forgive them,<br>for they should have known better." |
| All | *God, in your mercy,*<br>*help us remember.* |
| STATION 7 | The Crucified Land |
| WORD 7 | "Woman, behold your child" (John 19:25–27) |
| Leader | God, we hear the land crying, crying, crying:<br>"Why have you forsaken me?"<br>The land is crying like your son, crucified<br>by the very people who know the crucified one.<br>The original custodians of the land<br>have long felt the suffering of the land crucified, |

dispossessed, exploited, polluted.
Jesus Christ, God born of human clay,
are you suffering with the land still?
Mother Earth, can you hear God calling
calling you to look up to the cross,
with the words:
"Woman, behold your child."

All
*God, in your mercy,*
*help us remember.*
*Help us to hear you in the land.*
*Help us feel you in the clay.*
*Help us to love you in this Earth.*
*Help us remember.*

# REFLECTIONS AND READINGS

## OF ONE SUBSTANCE, by Robert Bos[1]

*"In him all things in the sky and on land were created . . . all things have been created through him and for him . . . in him all things hold together."* (Colossians 1:16–17)

at this moment
at every moment
I breathe in air
I breathe out air

the air I breathe
is also the air you breathe

we all share the same breath
the same molecules of air
we all share the same air
that which is part of you
and gives you life
is part of me
and gives me life

and not only we
but all people
and not only those alive now
but also those that once lived
and those who are yet to live

my breath is your breath
and everyone's breath

also all animals
share the same breath
what is at one moment me
is at the next moment
emu or turtle or parrot
and then is part of me again

the air we breath in
is breathed out by plants
what was me is now plant
and then me again

my body is mostly water
I drink water
from streams and rivers
I drink rain
and it becomes my body

what is at one moment me
is at the next moment you
and then creek
or tree
or kangaroo
or hail storm

water flows through me
and joins me
to all things

at every moment
I am part
of the great cycles of Earth
cycles of air
cycles of water
cycles of life

I am grasses
I am bloodwood
I am cockatoo
I am porpoise
I am river
I am wind
I am fire
I am Earth

God becomes human
God becomes matter
God becomes breath
God becomes water
God becomes animal
God becomes plant
that is what it means
for God to be human

at this moment
I breathe molecules of air
that God in Christ breathed

the water that is me
was once the body of Christ

every breath I breathe
is God's breath
every sip I drink
is God's blood
every morsel I eat
is God's flesh

the body of Christ
is actually
literally
of the same substance
as my body
the blood of Christ
is my blood

all things
are of one substance
with the breath of Christ

all things
are of one substance
with the blood of Christ

all things
are of one substance
with God in Christ

## SONG OF SOPHIA, by Dianne Bradley[2]

### Invocation

In the name of Sophia God, creating, redeeming, and sustaining.

### Sophia Calls

What thoughts and images stay with you, hold you, as we listen to the text of Proverbs 8? What sparks your imagination?

Do you, with me, hear not only Wisdom-Sophia telling us how it was, but how it is?

We hear Sophia call from the text: "Come! Look! I was there — from the beginning; there, playing in the dance of creation — with God, companioning God as a designer-weaver, an artisan-child: rejoicing, delighting, and being delighted in daily. Come!"

Sophia calls as the one in all and through all — the intrinsic and eternal thread of creation — in the establishment of the skies and in the fountains of the deep; in the setting of the limits to sea; and in the marking of the foundations of Earth.

### Sophia Rejoices

Sophia is *'amon*, the Hebrew word which we have translated as designer-weaver; we may also translate *'amon* as "artisan" and "child." The text paints a picture of creation as awesome cosmic play. Here Sophia, as artisan-child — in her role as designer-weaver — claims her authority as witness and participant and declares her nature, her way of being and of relating. How may we respond then to Sophia, who was and is God's daily delight, and who in turn delights and rejoices in God, in God's inhabited world, and in the human race?

Does she rejoice still in the human race, I wonder? I wonder why we haven't always remembered her song. Is she indeed still playing, singing,

---

2. The ideas in this reflection were compiled by Dianne Bradley, in collaboration with the Sophia liturgy group, in May 2001. Reprinted with permission. The reflection focuses on the text of Proverbs 8:21–31 and draws on Proverbs 8:17–20 and John 10:10. The authors also used ideas from Fritjof Capra's *The Web of Life* (London: Flamingo, 1997), and Elizabeth Johnson's understanding of the incarnation in *She Who Is* (New York: Crossroad, 1994), 150–51: "Christian faith is grounded on the experience that God who is Spirit at work in the tragic and beautiful world to vivify and renew all creatures through the gracious power of her indwelling, liberating love, is present yet again through the very particular history of one human being, Jesus of Nazareth." An alternative reflection, written by Norman Habel is included in the liturgy *Song of Sophia* (p. 93).

weaving, birthing, inspiring, and sustaining God's world, God's Earth, ourselves, and all Earth creatures?

## When We Stop and Look

Yes, of course we can see so much of Sophia at work — from the smallest of living things to the awesome wonder of the cosmos. If we have the heart and mind to see, we meet Wisdom-Sophia everywhere in the life of the world: in Queensland's wet tropical forests; in the Australian desert heart; in the rugged fragility of the Flinders Ranges; in our eclectic collections of what delights us in our suburban backyards, our gardens and parks. We meet her at the clothesline and at our kitchen tables. We meet Sophia where love and creativity births and sustains the way in which we, as human beings, relate to each other personally and in community. And, likewise, we meet Sophia in all that continues to birth and sustain Earth and Earth's ecological well-being.

In these places we do often remember . . . but we also forget. And what of the places where we do not find delight, those places of darkness and terror?

## Sophia Is Here Now

I was surprised to meet Sophia represented in a dark place. It was in 1998. I was at the National Gallery of Victoria in Melbourne, visiting the exhibition conceived and brought to fruition by Rosemary Crumlin, in her book *Beyond Belief*. There, in Anselm Keifer's painting *Lilit*, Sophia's image called out to me! Lilith was, according to Semitic mythology, Adam's first wife.[3]

There, moving between the splatters and explosions of gold, ochre, gray, and white — pressed against the soft lead background, intimating both catastrophe and alchemy's creative desire — was a lacy child's dress with trailing sashes. I was struck by this potent symbol of woman's survival and creativity in history in the midst of catastrophe. Here she is surviving the holocaust.

Even more wonderful for me was that Keifer's *Lilit* carried the strong remembrance of Sophia, of her creative impulse, of her transforming being in the eternally present, primordial, cosmic, chaotic dance.

---

3. "Lilit" is the German translation of the Hebrew name, translated as "Lilith" in contemporary English.

Sometimes it helps us when we remember that Sophia dwells in those awesome, dangerous places. In the midst of chaos, and at its edges, Sophia is forever weaving new patterns of life and death.

## Sophia Renews All Creation

Such renewed awareness calls into contrast our human forgetfulness and its consequences.

The scars of our forgetfulness are marked in our relationships — with each other, with God, and with God's inhabited world—wherever love's wisdom is absent.

At last we are beginning to see these scars for ourselves as we see the damage we are causing to this world. At last our minds are being opened to this forgetfulness. At last we are listening to the modern prophets speaking to us through contemporary ecology, science, and theology. Wisdom-Sophia is crying out to us through the words of her prophets. Is it too late?

For Wisdom-Sophia, it is never too late. She invites us to follow her way and have life in its fullness every day. Jesus-Sophia reminds us of Sophia's promise: Jesus also promises that we may have life, and have it abundantly. Jesus-Sophia reminds us that life is not about the salvation and the well-being of human beings in isolation from the rest of creation. Wisdom-Sophia reminds us that our well-being is intrinsically connected to the well-being of living Earth.

We are slowly learning that if we do not stop exploiting our planet, Earth, we will die. Earth has become less and less habitable for many species — and it can cease to be a home for us, too.

However, some scientists — as I learned recently to my surprise — are arguing that Earth is able to produce and sustain life despite us. It seems that the eternal nature of Sophia is discernible even in contemporary atheistic science. The Earth is once again being recognized as a living organism. This perception is not new to Indigenous peoples; modern Western science is coming to a new understanding of "feedback loops" that regulate Earth's processes just as we now know our own bodies are regulated.

For example, the regulation of carbon in the atmosphere seems to be connected with the natural weathering of rocks: rock dust, combined with rainwater, absorbs carbon from the air. Ultimately, the absorbed carbon is deposited as vast limestone sediments in the ocean. The elegant twist is that the weathering of rocks is facilitated by the action of bacteria, and bacteria are more active when the weather is warmer. So the "greenhouse effect" actually speeds up the inbuilt global remedial process!

Scientists and ecotheologians, recognizing the role of Wisdom-Sophia in creation, are engaging with the wisdom of first peoples and arguing that everything is interrelated: complex systems also sustain the living organism that is planet Earth and its atmosphere.

We are being called to respect and cooperate with these systems of relationship, this web of life. Can we not hear Sophia's call to wisdom here too? Do we not find her invitation attractive? Do we not wish to participate in the wonder of creation's cycles — of loving, suffering, dying, rising?

This is the abundant living to which Sophia-Jesus calls us. We now have the knowledge and the means to respond to our wounding of creation and to participate in Earth's healing, and our own healing. We, each in our own place, know what we need to mend in the patterns of our own lives and communities. We need only the will — the will to move from the weapons and ways of destruction to ways of life. So let us cherish the gift and wonder of creation.

If we do, maybe humanity will be there to witness and to celebrate all Earth's abundant living.

## Prayer

May we respond to Sophia's nature and to her call with our "yes."

May Sophia continue to rejoice in God's inhabited world and to delight in the human race.

Amen.

## EARTH MOTHER SPEAKS WITH HER BELOVED, by Colin Cargill[4]

The sun has gone down, my beloved; it is dark and my children are engaged in their night pursuits. The ancient story says that you were present at my appearing, when I came up out of the waters. It was a miracle — and not very different from the birth of a kangaroo or a human child! The

---

4. South Australian Council of Churches; reprinted with permission.

waters, our security for so long, parted and a new life appeared with all its infinite possibility. This is how I came to be; then you made me the mother of all Earth creations.

Do you remember the first creatures, those primitive little fish? How they had to struggle! I remember when the sun dried the waters and slowly it dawned on those creatures that they either found a way to walk or they died. Do you remember when those awkward little characters first stood up in the mud and began to "walk"? I will never forget their courage, their will to live.

Do you remember when I brought forth grass and flowers? What amazing little creatures! Flowers that pop their seeds all over the place; grass seeds picked up by the birds and spread everywhere. That was my greening time. That was when the birds began to sing in the morning, and I rejoiced with them.

The humans have been the most exasperating of my children. They were great at first: humble, open to the wonder of it all, taking only what they needed, treading lightly on my face.

But when they became more "civilized," they also became more destructive! You see these pock marks all over my face? They made them to extract what they call "precious stones." You see these great scars all over my skin? They called it "clearing." They used their tools to denude me and brother sun began to burn me. They created waste that polluted my skin; the salt in my body began to rise to the surface, and the life in my flesh began to ooze away.

I sometimes wonder if I am going to survive, my beloved. I want to cry out to you to do something. But I know you too well. You love them as you do all creation. You have given them freedom — and responsibility. You have kept your promise to love me; but they haven't. I can't take too much more of their abuse, my beloved.

Perhaps a mother must sometimes act to prevent the cruelties of her children. Perhaps, together, we can find a way to bring about reconciliation with our children. There is still time. Maybe then they will love me as a mother, and we will celebrate life together. And that would make it all worthwhile!